Nora
Nicholson
Chameleon's
Dish

Claudius: How fares our cousin Hamlet?

Hamlet: Excellent i' faith; of the chameleon's dish: I eat the air, promise-crammed. You cannot feed capons so.

Hamlet, III, 2

NORA NICHOLSON
CHAMELEON'S DISH

with a foreword by Sir John Gielgud

Paul Elek
London

FOR WENDY TREWIN
with love and gratitude

ISBN 0 236 15496 6

Published 1973 in Great Britain by
Elek Books Limited
54–58 Caledonian Road
London N1

Printed in Great Britain by A. Wheaton & Co., Exeter

Contents

Acknowledgements

I would like to thank Wendy and John Trewin, Veronica Silver and Alan Bennett for their invaluable help and advice during the writing of this autobiography, and the BBC, Michael Childers, Joe Cocks, Brian Hawksley, Raymond Mander and Joe Mitchenson, and the Rank Organization for their permission to reproduce photographs.

List of Illustrations

The Lady's Not for Burning in America, 1950, with John Gielgud and Pamela Brown. (Photo: Will Rappard)

Alma Taylor in *Comin' Thro' the Rye*, 1923. (Photo: Raymond Mander and Joe Mitchenson Theatre Collection)

Christopher Fry in recent years.

Virginia McKenna as Jean Paget with me as Mrs Frith in *A Town Like Alice*, 1956. (Photograph by courtesy of the Rank Organization)

Claire Bloom in *A Doll's House*, 1973. (Photo: Michael Childers)

Fay Compton as Aunt Ann, Fanny Rowe as Emily, Nora Swinburne as Aunt Hester and me as Aunt Juley in *The Forsyte Saga*, 1967. (Photo: BBC Television)

Relaxing during rehearsals for *Forty Years On* with Alan Bennett and Sir John Gielgud, 1968. (Photo: Brian Hawksley)

FOREWORD

Nora Nicholson. Never at liberty. Versatile, extremely talented. Spry, wonderful company, occasionally caustic. Observant, professional, indomitably energetic. Devoted friend. In her book she tells in her own delightful way of all the windings of her remarkable career, during which I have had the joy of knowing her from my very earliest beginnings in the theatre. Her heroes and heroines are mostly the same as mine, and how charmingly she remembers and writes about them.

Her attitude is perfectly up-to-date; her reverence for tradition, good manners and integrity never makes her narrow or old-fashioned. She is a tonic and an example, a rare possessor of faith, hope and charity. As Lady Bracknell remarked with characteristic firmness: 'What more can one desire?'

JOHN GIELGUD
March, 1973

I
VICTORIAN CHILDHOOD

Over my shoulder I look back on long years stretching behind me. Before embarking on this book I tried to recall my earliest memory. Not a particularly elevating one in any sense of the word. I was about three years old and on the nursery floor of my home at Svea Lodge, Leamington, banging my head in a paroxysm of rage.

I don't think I was an unnaturally violent child. It was simply a protest against life in general, which even at this early age presented problems: just an outlet peculiar to myself and carrying no Freudian significance as far as I know. This characteristic persisted in a modified form for many years. There was a wardrobe in my bedroom which testified to onslaughts from shoes, hairbrushes and other handy missiles. Nowadays perhaps I am not strong enough for such athletics.

Being the youngest of a large family I was alternately spoilt and teased by my elders. When promoted to take meals in the dining-room I was constantly intrigued and exasperated by the grown-ups' conversation in which, of course, I wasn't included. I used to console myself with the knowledge that the Wurri, our household cat, suffered from the same exclusion. The dread of being 'out of it' has pursued me right into old age, though now, I hope, tempered with a little forbearance.

At the same time I hated being talked down to. This made such a lasting impression on me that I've always been apt to treat youngsters as if they are my own age, and am rather gratified to find they seem to do the same with me. I used to call my sisters' patronising conversation being trotted to. This originated in their annoying habit of adjusting their strides to my small steps when out walking and the phrase is still included in the family vocabulary.

My father never trotted to me. He was one of the most enchanting companions of my childhood. He was incumbent of Saint Alban's Church, Leamington; one of the last churches, I believe, to be known as a Proprietory Chapel. After his death it was absorbed into the Parish of Leamington, and now I hear it has been demolished— I expect a block of offices or an hotel has been thrown up in its place. Whenever I happened to be passing through Leamington I always used to look out of the train window at the copper spire, and recall my childhood.

My father was Irish through and through. His maternal great-grandmother was one of the Butlers, descended from the first Earl of Ormond who could claim descent, on the distaff side, from Edward the First. I remember boasting of my Royal Lineage to one of my small friends —horrid little snob! Soon after being ordained my father came to England and never returned to his native Tipperary. I've never lived in Ireland but I am deeply aware of my Irish blood and whenever I set foot on Irish soil I think 'This is my own, my native land', although we own no property there now.

I believe my grandfather, Joseph Langrishe Nicholson, who lived in a house called Wilmar (derived from William and Mary) County Tipperary, was a hard man who gave his children little understanding or sympathy. Perhaps that accounted for the affection my own father always showed us. My grandmother was gentle and charming; devoted to her three sons. She is said to have sold the family diamonds in order to send them to Trinity College, Dublin where they did remarkably well. My father took a First Class in Divinity (and *ad eundem*, MA Oxford). He also received his diploma for LL.B. and LL.D. at Trinity College, Dubin and won the large gold medal. I regret to say that during a bad patch in the family fortunes, my sisters and I sold the gold medal for something like a mess of pottage. May we be forgiven.

My Uncle Horatio (also a clergyman) I met only once and didn't take to. He was an eccentric, dilettante person, reputed to preach in lavender gloves and possess an irascible temper. The legend that he hurled a rice pudding at one of his children during a lunch-time altercation is probably true. His family's reputation was as eccentric as his and my brief encounters with them only confirmed this picture.

My Uncle William, sometime Vicar of Egham and author of an odd little book, '*Questions and Answers*', was cast in much the same mould. He and his wife, Aunt Elizabeth, were notable Evangelicals. On hearing that my brother, H.O., had gone on the stage, my aunt exclaimed, 'How did they get hold of him?' Neither of my uncles seems to have shared my father's sense of humour nor his charm.

My father and mother were both romantics. The story goes that he was passing down Pulteney Street, Bath, when he spotted my mother, one of the Mayor's daughters, on the balcony of her house and said to his companion: 'That's the girl I'm going to marry'. I don't know how soon after that they became acquainted, but before long they were engaged. The scene of the engagement was a picnic at Limpley Stoke, near Bath, and the day was always kept as a family anniversary.

Not long ago someone whom I'd met for the first time described me as an outrageous flirt. At my age? Really! No, I'm simply a romantic, like my parents and certainly no flirt. Anyway I hate the word, smacking as it does of the Victorian Miss.

I don't remember a time when I wasn't in love. My first lover was named Hughie. I think we were aged about four and seriously in love. Where is he now? Picking flowers in the Elysian Fields? Or perhaps he's a white-haired grandfather. Our affair faded out and Hughie's place was taken by our family doctor for many years. I forget who succeeded him—probably one of my father's choirboys. Now that I'm an old woman and have ceased to have love affairs, I am still an incurable romantic.

My mother came of a large West Country family. Perhaps she derived her charm and vitality from her French grandmother. She was very beautiful; in her youth a sparkling brunette, but I knew her only when her hair was silver-grey. I think she brushed it about a hundred times a day until her old age. As a family we all went grey early. When I first went on the stage grey hair in a young person wasn't tolerated. I dyed my hair its original dark brown for years, and then just before the last war I settled down to being a grey-head. My mother's eyes, hazel, grey or brown according to her mood, had a disconcerting habit of searching yours as if they saw miles beneath the surface. I shrank under their scrutiny and my love for her was tainted by a pervading sense of guilt. Although in many ways indulgent, she maintained a strict discipline. Certain books were taboo, pocket-money restricted—I really do recall getting one halfpenny per week—friends were inspected.

Not only were certain books forbidden, there were numberless subjects—sex, of course, being predominant —which weren't mentioned. People talked in undertones about babies. Where did they come from? Never mind. If it hadn't been for an older girl who initiated me into the rudiments of childbearing, I might have reached maturity without knowing a thing about it. Now reticence has been superseded by an almost blatant parade of sex-consciousness. It may have its drawbacks but on the whole it's a blessing. Legs—even piano legs— no longer have to be concealed beneath frills and petti- coats, and bosoms flaunt with almost eighteenth century candour. At the same time, the spirit, at one time completely ignored, seems, in the present era, to be assuming some importance. The youth of today is reaching out for something beyond the body.

My mother's romantic nature was very endearing. Quite shortly before she died, well over eighty, she remarked about one of Ruby M Ayres' heroes, 'I think I'm rather in love with Hugh Stafford.' This trait

aps being allowed the thrill of meeting some of the
s after the show. I fell madly in love with Harcourt
ms, playing Edgar in *King Lear*. I wrote for and
ed his autograph which I wore next to my heart
onths, but we didn't meet until, a lifetime later,
ayed brother and sister in *The Lady's Not For
g*, and I continued to love him if not quite so
ately. But this is a digression. I must get back to
Lodge, where it all began.

Lodge was the name of our home: a comfortable,
house in an avenue of lime trees. The name 'Svea'
mething to do with Sweden where my father had
or seven years as British Chaplain in Gothenburg.
as a long time before my own appearance. Five
hildren were to precede me. My brother, H.O.,
aine, my eldest sister, were born in Gothenburg.
rought up on histories of the wonderful life my
lived over there. One of the high spots was a
which my mother danced with King Oscar; I
she made rather a hit with His Majesty, and as
name was Oscar I used to chaff my mother about
ntage. Even in those far off days children could
rtinent.

this romantic country my parents brought back
er of its customs. The table decorated with
little statues of the twelve apostles, and a
box with a train winding in and out of a tunnel
chanting tune—they all had their origin in
We even kept to the tradition of having our
on Christmas evening (and hung up our
on New Year's Eve instead of at Christmas).
s was a miraculous day. Church in the morning;
oon spent in packing our presents, and then,
we assembled in the dining-room with the
also present. After a breathless interval a
would make his entrance armed with a huge
ts. My father, laying aside the rigours of the
stmas Services, impersonated four different

coloured her attitude to all of us. I think she sub-
consciously resented the idea that any young man might
be more interested in her daughters than herself. She
kept a vigilant eye on Angela and then Constance when
they got engaged; even their love-letters didn't escape it.
I went through the same scrutiny when it was my turn.
But after a time my early fears evaporated and we
became the best of friends. I very often treated her
abominably—perhaps most of us trade on the affections
of our nearest and dearest—but she never bore malice
and was the most forgiving person I've ever known. She
was an avid reader, from the aforementioned Ruby M
Ayres to Gibbon's *Decline and Fall*. This proclivity she
shared with my father who, brilliant scholar though he
was, could occasionally immerse himself in my sisters'
women's magazines.

I adored my brothers and sisters—all a good few
years older than I—and respected their opinion to such
a degree that I became positively insincere in my desire
to please. After my father's death I was much drawn to
Catholicism but my dread of what The Others would
think prevented my doing anything about it beyond
sneaking down to the Catholic Repository to buy lurid
little pictures and statues, kept hidden away in my room.
My brothers Cyril and H.O. who were of course both
old enough to have been my father, were godlike in my
eyes. My two eldest sisters, Elaine and Angela, subjected
me to a lot of criticism, resented at the time, but today
I'm really grateful for it. They taught me at least the
rudiments of good manners. Constance, although several
years my senior, was my chum and only confidante.
We fought incessantly and I was intensely jealous of her
—she was a beauty and I wasn't—but our friendship
never faltered. One of her last words to me, the very day
she died, was, 'Little nursery friend.'

We four daughters shared two tremendous interests:
our love of the theatre and our love of scribbling. I
wrote my first story, an admonitory tale entitled '*Kate's

Disobedience', at the age of six. I was very backward in learning to write and my efforts were laboriously printed with the left hand. Fortunately for me, my parents didn't share the popular belief in the dire consequences of being left-handed, with the result that I became more or less ambidexterous.

I made further incursions into story-writing during the Boer War, an event which made scarcely any impact on our lives, and I have only very hazy memories of it, beyond looking out places on the map of Africa and listening to patriotic songs, such as *The Soldiers of the Queen*, on the sands at Weymouth. I was told the names of the generals, principally Lord Roberts, Redvers Buller (whose birthday was on December 7th, the same day as mine) and Hector Macdonald, known as 'Fighting Mac', whose photograph I cherished and made him the hero of one of my moral short stories. Years later I paid much the same homage to Lord Montgomery; hero-worship dies hard. The Boer War had its ups and its tragic downs. When at last it came to an end I can recall little of the national rejoicing, but I do remember after the Relief of Mafeking hearing the sound of cheers in the street below the nursery. Very few soldiers who fought in that war are living today; I believe there are still one or two veterans among the Chelsea Pensioners. I broke into verse about that time. One, in honour of Fighting Mac had the soul-stirring first line: 'Thou hero of a hundred fights'—the rest I have fortunately forgotten.

As for the theatre, I don't remember a time when my sisters weren't involved in theatricals. Even at an early age, when I was unwillingly made to hear them their lines, I privately scorned all this amateur stuff, and was determined to go on the stage properly and professionally. We had no theatrical background, although one of my mother's brothers, Uncle Joe, a barrister by profession, seems from his diaries, to have spent most of his time in amateur acting; I still have dozens of old photographs of him in various plays and costumes. The

only professional in our family was
to his friends as H.O. He joined th
when I was a small child and I re
feeling rather ashamed of his callin
period, being a Nonconformist, loo
the path to perdition. 'What do
inquired one of my mother's friend
'He's in business'. As the term 'b
connoted some sort of shop-keep
considered degrading, I wonder t
friend assigned him. I kept my ov
myself.

H.O. Nicholson is only a nam
ation and perhaps not even that
most outstanding actors of his d
of his age were looked upon
label him thus. He was a man
into his work a delicacy and
possibly stood in the way of h
tells me, 'Your acting reminds
regard it as high praise. As a
happy to have anything approa
gentleness.

For many years my theatre
annual pantomime at the Th
with occasional trips to Birmin
seeing Ada Reeve as Aladdi
eleven when I was taken to
of Venice, at Stratford-upon-
with the play and the thrill
the stage was an unforgetta
Leamington being only a fe
sisters and I used to bicycle
we could afford during th
hours in the gallery queu
striding in at the stage-door
watching the show. And, o
excitement of seeing one's

characters, each in turn dealing out the presents with suitable remarks addressed to each recipient. There was a German Professor, an Army Officer in resplendent uniform; I've forgotten the third, but the fourth was a disreputable old Irish woman named Mrs Muggins, wearing a revolting mask. She was the most garrulous of the quartet and had constant recourse to some commodity hidden beneath her shawl. I think the actor himself got as much fun out of it as any of us.

During the holidays the rest of us provided our own form of entertainment. We got up a species of variety show for the delectation of the household and one or two chosen friends. This consisted of songs, dances and one-act plays. It was my first incursion into play-acting and a terrifying experience it was. I didn't mind the dancing, I was rather good at that. In fact, the first press notice I ever had was in the *Leamington Courier* when I appeared in a *pas de deux* at an amateur performance of a fairy play. 'Little Miss N. Nicholson was particularly good', said the reporter. My nanny read it to me, to the annoyance of my mother who feared I'd become vain and was doubtless right. Constance was a born comedienne and played character parts without a tremor. I remember her singing the famous *Lincolnshire Poacher* in great style. My two grown-up sisters, Elaine and Angela, provided the more sophisticated items. The Svea Lodge drawing-room was about half the size of a small concert hall, and our audience consisted of a few chosen friends and the servants, those latter being the most appreciative.

Nearly all families on my parents' visiting list, however modest their income, boasted a staff of servants. My own family, though we couldn't have been well-off by any standards, kept at least four: Cook, a house-parlourmaid and two nannies, to say nothing of a jobbing gardener and a sad-faced cleaning-woman who came once a week. The other day I came across my mother's wages book and was scandalized. Twenty pounds per annum for cook, and about eighteen for the housemaid whose duties included carrying up immense brass cans of hot water from the basement to serve the grown-ups' daily hip-baths. I myself enjoyed this luxury only on Saturday nights, in front of the nursery fire; for the rest of the week I took a daily plunge into ice cold water. Perhaps this may account for my robust health in old age though I'm sure I should die if subjected to it now.

Nanny ruled over the nurseries, assisted by a succession of young girls whose menial duties consisted in taking up the nursery meals (about three flights of stairs) clearing away and being general dogsbody. All this labour for a mere pittance. Of course, the staff was well fed, decently if soberly clothed and apparently satisfied, judging by the length of time they stayed with us. Our cook stayed from my early childhood until I had grown up. She was distressingly deaf and unfailingly good tempered.

In all this hierarchy, Nanny was the chief character. One's whole life revolved round her. Any deviation from the pattern of nursery routine had more effect on me than the goings on of the rest of the household. I looked on the grown-ups as a kind of treat, especially my mother. She would come into the nursery to say good morning, take me out shopping on special occasions and then I'd see no more of her until the nightly half-hour in the drawingroom before bedtime. Then we played games and sometimes my father would come in and dance an Irish jig or join in charades. On rare occasions I would be allowed to sit in the hired victoria when my mother drove out to pay social calls. In those days ladies held what was known as At Home Days when stately friends would arrive for tea and they would leave visiting cards which filled a bowl on the hall table. Sometimes I was summoned to go round the room shaking hands with the guests and submitting with the utmost reluctance to kisses and patronising comments upon my lessons and how much I had grown. I hated being kissed by grown-up people. Remembering this I usually refrain from kissing young children: a species of being trotted to. Up in the nursery, surrounded by innumerable toys, I was blissfully free. But as a rule noisy play was frowned upon. My father's voice, coming up from the study, would demand, 'What is all that uproar?' Especially on Friday evenings we would be admonished, 'Don't make a noise, your Papa is writing his sermon.'

After my first beloved Nanny left us to be married, I was subjected to somewhat sterner stuff—'Brookie' whom I loved but feared. She was a strict Nonconformist and strongly disapproved of the ritual in my father's church, being committed, poor soul, to attend our Sunday Services. While helping my mother and sisters to dress for balls or theatres, her mouth would tighten and she would make gloomy predictions about their life in the world to come. Illness was another of her pet topics. I remember her saying to Constance, 'Don't press my arm, dear, something might form.' No wonder my sister grew up with an unreasoning horror of any kind of illness. The stories with which Brookie used to vary the monotony of our daily walks usually started with the ominous preface of 'A man at my home . . . and ended up with the horrific climax . . . and he went raving mad.'

When I was a little older I was promoted to a 'Children's Maid', a darling person called Roberts, known to us as 'Pob'. She became a playmate with a complete absence of disapproval. Thus my childhood passed, and though I absorbed a certain amount of general knowledge, I learnt nothing domestically useful. When I went to boarding school I didn't even know how to plait my hair much less mend my clothes or fold them up at bedtime.

The high spot of my early years was the annual summer holiday. My parents rented part of a house in Weymouth and we stayed there for six or seven weeks. The sun seemed to shine perpetually. There were countless amusements: donkey-rides (threepence a go and sixpence for a lengthy session), sand castles on the glorious beach and bathing every day. For me the indignity of only paddling until I was old enough to start swimming. The donkeys used to stand in their special corner, bearing their own cross and waiting patiently to bear the heavier cross of human bodies. We had our particular favourites, Young Violet and Old Violet (the latter usually assigned to me as the youngest of the family). How I used to long to mount Peter, a brunette with reputedly vicious tendencies, said to have thrown many a daring rider. Then there were the goat-carriages, a means of locomotion that most of us despised. The story goes that Angela, demanding a donkey, shouted the alternative, 'If not, a goat.' 'If not, a goat' has come to connote any kind of inferior alternative. The slogan is used not only by the family but has been adopted by many of our friends.

Bathing in those days was conducted from a strange horse-drawn vehicle called a bathing-machine, a sort of little wooden hut with steps at either end. I think the cost was about sixpence which you paid into the hand of a much tanned and wrinkled person known as the Bathing-woman. You ascended into a dim compartment smelling of seaweed and damp towels and were driven out to sea. Having donned a bathing-suit, designed for modesty rather than elegance, you descended more steps and found yourself at sea, sometimes neck-deep. The more intrepid swam out boldly; my own memories are of clinging to a rope and bobbing up and down in a state of mingled delight and fear.

Another enormous attraction was the Pierrots. They held daily concerts on the sands and we sat around, joining in the choruses and swooning with joy if one of us was picked out for special attention. There was a rival entertainment, if such it could be called, in the daily session, also on the sands, of a religious society known as the Children's Special Service Mission. I believe it still exists. The Mission was conducted by an enthusiastic bearded gentleman named Josiah Spiers. Any kind of dramatic entertainment was anathema in his eyes; I don't know how I reconciled my adored Pierrots with my conscience, but the influence of Mr Spiers induced me to include in my daily prayers the petition that I might be prevented from going to the Christmas pantomime. I'm afraid the petition wasn't sufficiently earnest, for the following Christmas found me an enthralled spectator.

In those days Weymouth was beautiful, with its Georgian houses and narrow streets. One of the greatest treats was going to the Garrison church and watching the red-coated soldiers being marched off to barracks after Morning Service. At one time my eldest brother Cyril was stationed at Weymouth and we had the added thrill of seeing him commanding his men. And then, on a dim September evening, we were home again and Svea Lodge greeted us as strangers. The sun retreated and winter set in.

Taken as a whole my early childhood was sheer bliss. The tangled garden with its profusion of red may, lilac and the one laburnum tree I was allowed to climb was my constant playground. Here I often played in solitude but I was never really alone. My world was peopled with imaginary beings far more alive than the people around me. I invented a school whose pupils were of high degree and vastly talented. I have the record still of the teachers, pupils, their places in class and all the school activities. They included such names as Olympia Langrishe (a family name of ours), Sybil de Trafford and Mona Disraeli, and I made out a programme of their performance of *As You Like It*.

Although my reading was under fairly strict supervision, the nursery bookshelves were full of entertainment. Mrs Molesworth, first favourite with the children of my day; Mrs Ewing; Louisa M Alcott whose *Little Women* I still know by heart, and every variety of children's magazine. Many of the stories bore an admonitory flavour, notably such epics as *The Wide, Wide World* and *Ministering Children*. L. T. Meade was another favourite.

Her heroines were nearly always the children of rich parents: purses, stuffed with golden sovereigns, were often stolen by the villainess of the piece. *The Prisoner of Zenda*, more adult reading, I loved best of all, and to this day I make a point of re-reading it every two years without fail. One memorable summer stands out in continuous sunshine with an orgy of reading, from *Oliver Twist* to Thackeray's *Book of Snobs*. H.O. was at home on one of his rare visits and I was given the heavenly task of hearing him his lines as Feste in *Twelfth Night*. Perpetually halting over unpronounceable words, I was encouraged by his admonitory, 'On, wee-voice, on!' and *Twelfth Night* has remained one of my most beloved plays.

From an early age I adored dressing up and impersonating my own imaginary characters. My greatest triumph occurred when I called on my mother, arrayed in one of her own dresses, my youthful features disguised by drawing a veil tightly over my face and assuming an elderly voice. I think I was supposed to be touting for some charity. I was rather alarmed when my mother said graciously, 'Would you like to speak to Dr Nicholson?' I replied swiftly, 'No, thank you.' Anyway, my mother was most polite, presented me with two shillings and saw me to the front door with many expressions of good will. There was much laughter when I threw off my disguise, but I was obliged to return the ill-gotten two shillings, which I thought very unfair.

There were many other exploits later on, chiefly to vary the monotony of being out of work. One in particular might have had serious consequences. I was living at the time with the Pelissiers. Constance Pelissier, niece of Harry Pelissier (famous in those days for his concert party, *The Follies*) was my great chum in the Benson Company, and while my mother was off on a trip to New Zealand, I was a paying guest at her parent's home. Well, one afternoon, having procured a very dubious dress from a second-hand clothes shop, I called at the front door, ostensibly selling shoe-laces. I had great difficulty in persuading the parlourmaid to recognise me and allow me into the house. I had become uncomfortably aware of a number of curious people gathering outside the garden gate. While upstairs, getting myself back to normal, I was horrified by the sight of a policeman striding up the garden path. Sheepishly I presented myself and assured him that nothing nefarious had been going on. He went away, but I felt he wasn't entirely convinced of my sanity and he was probably right. I was terrified lest a paragraph might appear in the local paper but mercifully nothing came of that rather dangerous adventure. Another impersonation very nearly had me engaged as a house-parlourmaid to a wealthy family in Bayswater. It was only by inventing a previous application that I escaped being formally committed. The amount of work expected of me was unbelievable. The lady didn't invite me to sit down or see me to the door, and the interview almost turned me into a Communist.

Finally, in the heyday of the popular film star, Stewart Rome, I invented a lovesick maiden called Dorothy Maitland, and conducted a correspondence with him in which she declared her love. The unsuspecting film star responded with such sweet and kindly advice that I repented bitterly and, writing as Dorothy's aunt, told him that Dorothy had unfortunately died. An episode which causes me to bow my head in shame. Nowadays I'm more or less reconciled to retaining my own personality, unsatisfactory though it may be. 'To thine own self be true' is a sound maxim.

I recall another adventure of which I'm also a bit ashamed. During one period of unemployment I and another out-of-work friend used to frequent the Law Courts. Any kind of case was exciting but our special favourite was the Dennistoun Case, which involved the elegant Mrs Dennistoun. I can't remember the details but it was something to do with unpaid bills. Marshall

Hall, defending the case, was taken ill and his deputy was a certain Norman Birkett, brilliant but more or less unknown. My chum and I were spellbound by his rhetoric but his slight Midland accent caused us some concern. With the arrogance and impertinence of youth, I took it upon me to call at his chambers, bearing a letter setting out a few of what I considered his imperfections. We were received by his clerk who politely read the letter and more or less engaged to show it to his chief. Certainly the offending accent disappeared as time went on, but I can't flatter myself it was due to my importunities. To have dared to approach the future great Lord Birkett was a presumption devoutly to be deplored.

II

SORROWFUL REALITY

My father was the strongest influence in my young life. His personality was the most vivid I have ever known. In writing of him now, his presence is as clear-cut as it was in his lifetime. With his powerful Irish rhetoric he could hold a congregation spellbound for an hour or more. What would his reception be in these days of ten-minute discourses, I wonder?

Of all listeners no one was more attentive than his youngest daughter. Sitting in the front pew, my mother's hand tightly held, I would drown in the music of his voice which never quite lost its Irish cadence; my ears intent on the words though not by any means on their substance, so that when at bedtime I would murmur, 'I loved your sermon this morning,' I would be gravelled for lack of an answer to his pleased 'What was it you liked best?' But while in the home circle he was the most accessible companion, in church he became an entirely different person with an eagle eye on any lapse from good behaviour. Not infrequently I'd be confronted with the question, 'Were you *laughing* in church this morning?' Doubtless I'd been exchanging grins with the choirboys. There was one in particular who, through all the years, has remained one of my most loyal friends. Every year, on the anniversary of my father's death, I receive a letter recalling bygone days which I don't suppose anyone else can remember so clearly.

How vividly those services at Saint Alban's stand out in my memory. Especially the Morning Service at Easter: a burst of triumphant chords on the organ, and then the entrance of the choir, the boys in blue cassocks and carrying little bunches of primroses, as they proceeded round the church to the strains of 'Jesus Christ is risen today' with the congregation singing their hearts out. Resurrection Morning *in excelsis*.

My father's organist Mr West, was responsible for my weekly piano lesson. He was a magnificent organ player but the piano was not his *forte*, if I may so express it. I was an exasperating pupil. I rarely applied myself to what he called 'private pragdis', and every week he would remark patiently, 'There's no occasion to *thump*, Miss Nixon' and proceed to give an example of the most outrageous thumping a piano has ever endured. My sister Angela, herself a superb pianist, was deputed to supervise my 'private pragdis' and for the time being we were implacable enemies, but later on we used to play duets together in perfect harmony—if such a word can be applied to my struggles as a very inadequate accompanist. Later at school I achieved modest acclaim for my playing, but I was an erratic performer and, though music has always an immediately soothing effect on my savage breast, it hasn't done much for my fingers.

Diction, known in those days as elocution, played a large part in my father's tuition. From my earliest years I used periodically to take my stand at one end of the study while, from the other end, he would direct me in such poetic effusions as *John Littlejohn*, having first settled the correct speech register by repeating 'Yes' several times. John Littlejohn was a person of repugnant virtue. His eulogy went something like this:

> 'John Littlejohn was stout and strong,
> Upright and downright, scorning wrong.
> Whenever a rascal strove to pass,
> Instead of silver, a coin of brass,
> John took his hammer and said with a frown,
> "The coin is spurious, nail it down." '

You can understand why I hated him and always broke into tears when coerced into reciting to an indifferent audience.

Tears or no, these were wonderful times. But after a serious illness I developed a 'temperament' and became subject to bouts of depression, unusual in so young a person; sometimes they were almost suicidal. Once, when staying at the seaside with my old nanny and her husband, and dogged by terrible homesickness, I peered over the cliffs and thought it might be no ill thing to take a header into the sea.

My illness was vaguely attributed to over-work. This sounds fantastic, but my father, a born teacher, had taken on himself the task of educating me and, finding me a responsive pupil, had forgotten my tender years. His weekly Scripture lessons were masterly but miles above my head, and my heart would sink as I watched him writing 'Agenda' at the top of my next week's homework.

After my illness things were toned down a little, but I think I learned more in those formative years than in all my later tuition at school.

When I was considered to have imbibed enough of my father's teaching I went for a year or two to the Leamington High School. I enjoyed a splendid time there, working as little as possible except during exams when I would wake in the early mornings and swot up the subjects out of which—most unfairly—I came pretty well. They were bright summer mornings with birds in full song and the scent of limes drifting in through the night-nursery window, while I lay on my stomach and repeated English dates and French verbs. I made lots of friends and indulged in the usual intermittent bouts of *schwämerei* for older girls and even the boys at Leamington College. English composition was my favourite subject. We were taught by M P Willcocks, later to become a well-known author, and a grand teacher she was. She once remarked, 'Nora Nicholson writes perfect English', which puffed me up beyond bearing. But I was ruthlessly deflated when I went to boarding-school and my English was pronounced affected. I was always striving after 'style', tried to imitate my favourite authors and developed a florid and no doubt turgid method which was swiftly censured by my English mistress. At this time of my life I was taking it very seriously and a somewhat priggish religious tone pervaded my writing.

At home the religious atmosphere wasn't oppressive. Apart from family prayers and compulsory attendance at church twice on Sundays, we enjoyed a certain amount of latitude. My father was regarded as High Church but by present-day standards, when Anglicanism is *plus Catholique que le Pape*, the ritual at Saint Alban's would be considered anaemic. He was thoroughly grounded in the Roman Liturgy, as he was to prove by a controversial correspondence with Cardinal Manning, which was published as a pamphlet. I can't now remember the title and anyway it happened long before my time. He was mad about Shakespeare, even to the extent of publishing a book called *No Cypher in Shakespeare*, being the refutation of a great cryptogram by the Honourable Ignatius Donnelly. For this achievement my father was presented with an illuminated address of appreciation from his parishioners—I wonder what became of it.

But there was a light and almost childlike side to his character, specially portrayed in the annual family lunch called The Girls' Sickening Feast, an event that took place during my mother's visit to London to see her sisters who, being Roman Catholics, weren't considered suitable guests at Svea Lodge. The feast itself consisted of gluts of strawberries and cream and was known as the GSF (as opposed to the Girls' Friendly Society). My mother would have been horrified at the amount we put away; my father enjoyed it as much as we did. We all made speeches, duly recorded, and after lunch retired to the study where my father wound up the proceedings by reading aloud an extract from Cicero's *Life of Caesar*. I've forgotten the exact quotation but it ended up, '. . . . Having taken a vomit. . . .', but I can vouch that the effect of the GSF had no such dire consequences.

All this sounds discursive but I want to give some idea of my father's character, its lovable mixture of gravity and fun. The long sessions when he read me Shakespeare had a lasting effect on my life in the theatre. He would bring the poetry to life so that even my youthful intelligence could grasp some of its beauty. What an actor he would have made! His very appearance was dramatic. The sparkle in his eyes, his white hair brushed up on each side of his face in what we used to call 'twigs', his slight, almost boyish figure would have graced any nineteenth-century stage. But although he enjoyed going to the theatre, like many Victorians he did not entirely approve of it: never once, for example, did he go to see H.O. in a play.

My father was reading *King Lear* to me a few weeks before he died. Even his death was dramatic. On a hot summer day my mother and I were at lunch and he was in his room, dressing for his first day out after a severe bout of influenza. I can still hear the thud of his falling body in the room above. In five hours he was dead.

He was greatly loved in the town and was given a public funeral. I remember the long procession of clergy and the mourning carriages, one of them containing Constance and myself, accompanied by Uncle William who quoted Shakespeare on the way, with what seemed to us extreme irreverence and irrelevance, but which would, I'm sure, have amused the beloved father now heading the procession in silent pomp.

Soon after my father's death we moved into a smaller house, still bearing the name of Svea. At first there was an idea that we should leave Leamington, but we stayed on, to my personal disappointment, as I was always eager for change of scene, and Leamington with its air of smugness and the sluggish river, significant of its inhabitants, had begun to pall. I was, however, accorded a slight change, being sent to boarding-school at Bournemouth. The delightful, lazy days at the High School were replaced by a couple of years' strict discipline and acute misery. I decided that God had a down on me and once again indulged in thoughts of suicide.

It isn't easy to imagine that particular school. Of course, the whole character of girls' schools has been revolutionised since my day, but I do maintain that mine was unique. Writing now of more than half a century ago, I can recall, as though it were last week, the restricted atmosphere of that select establishment. Accustomed as I was to the freedom of the High School, and my own home where I was petted and made much of, this new regime was completely alien. At that time my interests were almost equally divided between the theatre, writing and religion. Too consciously 'highbrow' for the more light-hearted of my schoolmates, too introspective for my own peace of mind, I hovered between being admired by the few, scarcely noticed by the majority and really detested by one or two. Consequently the first year at boarding school was really unhappy. How often have I refuted that aphorism 'The happiest days of your life'. I believe most of my wretchedness stemmed from my headmistress. She was a woman of small stature and immense dignity, with an inordinate sense of class. Nothing delighted her more than a title in your family. Any claim of mine to that distinction was so far removed as to be negligible, so I was out of the running there. But that wasn't why she disliked me. Because she did and the dislike was reciprocated. I was untidy, irresponsible and unprepossessing. My stockings were undarned, my blouses lacked buttons, my hair was in tangles. 'You'll kill your children', said one of the mistresses, tearing off my unaired blouse. I was supposed to have a fairly good brain but my other assets were all liabilities. I was nearly expelled for organizing a midnight feast (biscuits and lemonade) and my incurable tendency to ridicule my colleagues, not to mention my superiors, came in for censure. On my very last morning I was summoned to the Presence. There she sat in her study, an upright figure (five feet nothing but she gave the impression of an Amazon). She accorded me a long look down her long nose. 'Nora dearie,' she began. She invariably addressed us with that infuriating term of endearment. 'Nora dearie, I do wish you would be more sincere.' What did that imply? One of my more heinous bouts of ridicule had come to her ever-open ears. Some day, she warned me, I might find myself in a Court of Libel. With this admonition ringing in my ears, I left school, rejoicing and unrepentant. Perhaps my horrid fate is still to come.

But the year before I left had begun to look up through the arrival of Brynhild Benson, Frank Benson's daughter. We started a friendship which has endured to the present day when we still laugh over the school's enormities. How ridiculous and innocent it all was. We lived an almost conventual life. Anything male was looked upon with suspicion. Our music master's weekly visits were chaperoned by one of the staff. I can't believe that the unfortunate man could have derived the smallest temptation from his pupils with their unimaginative uniform and decorous coiffure, and even less from the Mademoiselle or Fraülein knitting demurely in her corner. However, *faute de mieux*, we were all in love with him and looked forward to his visits with tremulous excitement.

But with the advent of Brynhild, known to her family and to me as 'Dick', my horizon widened and I was eventually admitted into the bosom of the adored Benson family. I used to spend holidays with them at Stratford-upon-Avon and was sometimes allowed to watch a rehearsal. I would picture myself as some day included in that illustrious Company.

During the Company's visits to the Theatre Royal, Bournemouth, we were taken to see one or two plays, and on one occasion when they were playing *Hamlet*, H.O. took me backstage to be presented to my two idols for the first time. 'Now for Heaven's sake,' said he, 'don't go telling him he was good.' As if I'd have dared! Mr

31

Benson, beautiful and solemn in his suit of sables, gave me 'Good-day' as if I'd been a VIP and then seemed to forget my presence. Mrs Benson was altogether different. She took me to her heart and there I remained for the rest of her life. She was the most enchanting person, nothing aloof about her, while there was something royal about Mr Benson that gave you the feeling of being perpetually on your knees. But more of this hereafter. Lady Benson, as she afterwards became, had something deliciously childlike about her that somehow brought our ages together. Long after I had left the Company I used to stay in her house in Kensington and for a short while did a little secretarial work for her. But it is as a sweet and merry companion that I think of her most. When she was writing one of her novels and I was as usual scribbling away at some story or other, we would sit on either side of the fire, silent and absorbed, with an occasional interruption when she would ask me how to spell something, and that of course made me feel delightfully superior. As an actress she wasn't in the top class but as a teacher she had few equals. In my early days at the Old Vic she directed *She Stoops to Conquer* and from her I learned the importance of repose and economy of gesture, and some of the airs and graces of the eighteenth century.

While still at school I dared to confide in Mr Benson my ambition to go on the stage and received no encouragement. Book-learning was what he considered my forte. But that had no effect. An actress's life for me.

In the meantime, after leaving school, I grew up and 'came out'. This was an occasion of some ceremony, involving white satin and long gloves. Very different from those children's parties where I was never allowed to stay to the end but was bustled off wrapped in ignominy and a Shetland shawl, while more privileged youngsters were still enjoying the fun. (Then home in a bath-chair, a strange man-drawn vehicle, in those days a popular means of transport for young and old.) Now of course I could dance all night and no questions asked, except that my mother always insisted on scrutinizing my programmes, with raised eyebrows if the same name occurred more than three or four times. Encouraging young men was said to be 'cheap'. But I enjoyed myself for all that and went through numerous romantic encounters. I played lawn-tennis indifferently, endured a few bridge-parties which I hated, and paid occasional visits to the Theatre Royal.

Then I was sent to Germany for six months. I stayed with a family living in a beautiful old house in Brebach, a village near Saarbrücken. They were charming people and treated me like one of themselves, so much so that they allowed themselves to be embarrassingly frank about my country and its customs. Of course the prospect of war was far from our thoughts; our countries were the best of friends, even if 'Old England' occupied a slightly inferior position. Our hospitals were inadequate, we neglected our poor and were pathetically behindhand in music and housekeeping. As I myself was a wretched needlewoman and hadn't the sketchiest culinary knowledge, I wasn't a successful ambassador for my country.

It was winter time and there were sleigh-rides over the snow-laden countryside, skating on the lake and, of course, a wonderful Christmas tree and marvellous presents. All my declared wishes were fulfilled. There were numerous guests. The one I remember most vividly is Reinhold von Wahrlich, celebrated in those days for his beautiful baritone voice. He often gave recitals in London; his interpretation of Schubert's *Winterreise* was unforgettable. He was a fascinating man with glittering grey eyes. He spoke perfect English and this alone would have attracted me, thirsting as I was for the sound of my own language. I made him my confidant, and found that he understood something of my homesickness, my daydreams and bewilderment about life. In my autograph album, a cherished fetish of my generation, he inscribed a maxim I've always remembered: '*Lebet nicht am Schein, sondern in der tiefen wenn auch traurigen Wirklichkeit.*' Which roughly translated means: 'Don't live in make-believe but in the deep, if also sorrowful, reality.' I don't know who the author was, but his words were a timely warning to a romantic young person.

My homesickness was increased by the Sunday Services at the Lutheran Church. After one or two visits I gave up and took myself down the country lanes to the Catholic Church—my first experience of going to Mass. I don't think it made a serious impression on me beyond giving me a feeling of warmth, as approximating more nearly to Saint Alban's than the rigours of the Lutheran doctrine.

I acquired a certain amount of German, a language I came to love, especially where singing is concerned. In those days I had a fairly good mezzo-soprano voice—lost now, alas. I became more reconciled to the strange life, but with the coming of spring I returned home with an exquisite sense of release. My sister Elaine met me in Brussels where we spent a few ecstatic days, going to picture galleries and the Opera. I've often wondered what became of that dear German family. There was a small nephew, Wolfram, too young to have fought in 1914 but maybe he served in Hitler's war. I hope he survived. The families exchanged letters for some years but they faded out after a while.

Soon after my return home, our family fortunes being at a low ebb, my mother decided that a short sojourn in Bruges, where living was cheap, might reinforce them. This was a delightful break. We lived in a Pension, inhabited by all sorts of English people, most of them like ourselves slightly impoverished, but we managed to have quite a gay time. There were dances, amateur theatricals (which I enjoyed in spite of that stigma) which took us to Antwerp with the *Prisoner of Zenda*. There was weekly opera, concerts and a dramatic club at which we read Shakespeare—strictly bowdlerized by the chaplain's wife; 'Take up the bastard' she modestly rendered as 'Take up the infant'.

We spent nearly a year in Bruges: in those days completely unspoilt, a beautiful little city dominated by the Belfry with its bells chiming a different tune every quarter hour. I was supposed to improve my schoolgirl French but as most of my friends were English I didn't make much headway. I also fell in love again. He was a great deal older than I, and I think my feeling for him was largely youthful infatuation. There was another slight obstacle. He was married already and my mother, quite rightly, intervened and whisked me back to England where I proceeded to forget all about him, and doubtless he did the same about me.

III

THE BENJON COMPANY

And now I was all set for my assault on Mr Benson. I prevailed upon him to give me an interview in his dressing-room at the little old Memorial Theatre which was destroyed by fire in 1926; its large and imposing successor fails, for me at least, to hold the glamour of that small and quite ugly building. There are just a few remains left; I think the Museum is more or less intact.

My interview was a solemn occasion. I was back in church with my father's professional eye on me. Mr Benson loomed enormous to my frightened senses. I plunged into the Potion Scene from *Romeo and Juliet*, followed it with a bit of Maria in *Twelfth Night* and came to a full stop. Mr Benson gave me a faraway look from his luminous grey eyes and said nothing for a long time. Then he murmured, 'It might be worth your while', with which encouraging remark the interview ended. But it bore results.

For the sum of forty pounds I was enrolled as a student in the Benson School. I was to start in September, at the opening of the autumn tour. For most of that hot summer my mother had rented a small house at Shottery, a mile or two outside Stratford. We spent the days in the garden or on the river and went to the theatre nearly every night. How I loved watching from the stalls and looking forward to the time, only a few weeks distant, when I'd be on the right side of the foot-lights myself. And as the *bonne bouche* of that rapturous time, needless to say I fell in love again. He was a very junior member of the Company. Neither of us had any money and heaven knows at what distant period we could have married. I didn't even have a ring. When we announced our engagement to my mother she expressed instant disapproval, partly due, I was sure, to the fact that she'd not been in on it. Anyway, the whole thing was nipped in the bud, but for that short time I was more intensely happy than I'd ever been before—or since, for that matter. Shortly afterwards my mother sailed for New Zealand to stay with Elaine who was teaching dramatics out there, so I felt free to conduct my life as I wished.

I don't think there has ever been anything quite like the Benson School. All the other drama schools had their headquarters in London. We travelled with the Company, spent our mornings in class (drama, diction, dancing and fencing), attended rehearsals, when needed, and walked on at night—usually seven plays per week. My father's readings came in useful; I was familiar with most of the plays. Our training was first class. We were sent on for ladies-in-waiting, fairies and screaming mobs in *Julius Caesar*. I even portrayed a dead woman in *Coriolanus*. Potential stars—Henry Ainley, Matheson Lang, Oscar Asche and his wife, Lily Brayton, and Harcourt Williams, to say nothing of my own brother—had graduated from the Company long before my time. All the same we boasted a pretty fine galaxy; Baliol Holloway, who taught me how to do a character make-up, Dorothy Green, our leading lady (Mrs Benson had left the Company before I joined) and Murray Carrington and his wife Ethel, who became dear friends of mine. Dennis Neilson-Terry, my own contemporary, was sent by his father, Fred Terry, to learn his job at the feet of out Chief. None of these actors are alive now, but the children of some of them carry on the tradition, notably Gwynne Whitby, whose father, Arthur, was a magnificent actor. For us Old Bensonians their names will never die.

I wish I could explain the alchemy of Frank Benson's teaching. As an actor he came behind many of the youngsters he nursed into fame, but as a director he was unparalleled. He would stride into rehearsals, start operations with shouts of 'Breath, breath, breath!'—

Myself when young

My mother and father

My brother, H. O. Nicholson, as Starveling in the *Dream*.

The Benson Company around 1900: Frank Benson as Petruchio, Mrs Benson as Katharina, Murray Carrington as Lucentio in *The Taming of the Shrew*.

THEATRE ROYAL
Bradford
December 2nd to 7th, 1912.

THE PROGRAMME AT 7.30 P.M.

Monday
ANTONY AND CLEOPATRA

Tuesday   JULIUS CÆSAR

Wednesday
THE MERRY WIVES OF WINDSOR

Thursday
ANTONY AND CLEOPATRA

Friday   THE RIVALS (Sheridan)

Saturday (at 7.15 p.m.)
THE MERCHANT OF VENICE

MATINEE at 2 p.m.

Saturday
AS YOU LIKE IT

PRICES OF ADMISSION :
Private Boxes, £1 10s. ; Dress Circle, first 3 rows, 4s., 4th
and 5th rows, 3s. ; Orchestra Stalls, 4s. ; Pit Stalls, 2s. ;
Pit, 1s. : Gallery, 6d. Early Doors : Evenings, 6.45 p.m. ;
Saturday, 6.30 p.m. : Matinee, 1 p.m.—6d. extra to all
parts, including Gallery. Ordinary Doors : Evenings,
7.15 p.m ; Matinee, 1.30 p.m.
BOX OFFICE open daily from 9 a.m. to 5.30 p.m. Telephone No. 245.

The F. R. BENSON
SHAKESPEAREAN COMPANY

WILL INCLUDE

F. R. BENSON	JOHN MACLEAN
F. RANDLE AYRTON	DOROTHY GREEN
HARRY CAINE	ROSA BURGESS
MURRAY CARRINGTON	VIOLET CECIL
FRANK COCHRANE	MARION FOREMAN
RUPERT L. CONRICK	ETHEL McDOWALL
RIBTON HAINES	A. P. NICHOLSON
BALIOL HOLLOWAY	NORA NICHOLSON
JOHN HOWELL	CONSTANCE PELISSIER
JAMES MAGEEAN	EVE TITHERADGE
FRANK MATTHEWS	

Stage Manager	-		F. Randle Ayrton
Musical Director	-	For The	Alfred Spaelson
Advance Manager	-	F. R. BENSON	Charles Bosley
London Representative		Shakespearean	Henry Tossell
Assistant Manager	-	Company	Hugh Gwyther
General Manager	-		W. H. Savary

'Fixture' programme of the Benson Company, designed like a cricket
card, 1912.

*with love
from
Nora.*

Puck, with the Benson Company, 1912.

Fred Terry and Julia Neilson
in *Sweet Nell of Old
Drury*, 1900.

Dame Sybil Thorndike and
Sir Lewis Casson in
recent years.

Ernest Milton in *Night's Candles* (*Lorenzaccio*), 1933.

aimed at some panting student—hit upon a faulty inflexion and more than likely spend half the morning correcting it, and then stroll through his own part, littering it with astonishing paraphrase and highly original punctuation. But when it came to interpreting a part for someone else, here was magic. I can still remember his faultless portrayal of Puck, at rehearsal, with myself struggling to imitate him. I found no teacher to equal him until I came under the direction of Lewis Casson and Tyrone Guthrie, twenty years' later. They didn't teach you how to act, they taught you to *be*. A young actress of my acquaintance, cast for an old woman, implored Edith Evans to tell her how to approach the part. 'You don't have to *act* an old woman,' she said, 'Just *be* an old woman.' Easier said than done, but of course that is the secret of acting: to *be*. Dame Edith herself is a shining example of *being*.

Benson rehearsals started usually at eleven as against the ten or ten-thirty of today. Ten minutes' grace was given, to allow for differences in clocks and watches, but abuse of this concession led to a fine of half-a-crown. No mid-morning coffee-breaks but at about half past twelve Richmond, Mr Benson's faithful valet and henchman, made an entrance loaded with bagfuls of buns with which the actors could assuage their hunger and impair their diction. During the Stratford Festivals quite often there would be a call after the show at night; not surprising when you realise that, apart from the weekly itinerary, there might be at least two revivals. One was *Antony and Cleopatra*, in which Dorothy Green gave her unforgettable performance of Cleopatra, and I, a humble student, walked on in various guises.

When, as a schoolgirl, I first met Frank Benson, I considered him elderly. I suppose he was actually well into middle-age, though still rather apologetically play-ing Romeo. By the time I joined the Company, Murray Carrington had succeeded him in romantic leads, and Benson played the parts he probably most enjoyed. As

Caliban he swung from trees, munched revolting-looking fish and somehow contrived to be both funny and moving. He looked savage and magnificent as Macbeth, but in common with most actors he wasn't altogether successful. I don't think I have ever seen a really satisfying Macbeth. In John Gielgud's production during the last war, his 'Tomorrow' speech exceeded everyone else's in beauty and pathos, but even he wasn't ideal for he never quite suggested the warrior. I remember in *The Lady's Not For Burning* he seemed to be poet turned soldier, whereas Alec Clunes, who created Thomas Mendip at the Arts Theatre, was emphatically soldier first and poet a long way after.

Benson's Richard the Second has always been considered his best part. He had eulogies from C E Montagu and James Agate, and my own memories of his performance are still quite vivid, though all Richards must come behind John Gielgud's superb portrayal. My chief remembrance of Benson's Hamlet is that in the Play Scene he used to recline on the stage, his back to the audience, and try very effectively to make me laugh while I wrestled with 'For us and for our tragedy'. I've always suffered from a distressing tendency to giggle on the stage, or in modern parlance, to 'corpse'. By now I have overcome it to a certain extent, but there are still moments when I have a fight to keep serious. There are certain actors and actresses, dear friends of mine, who are a torment to act with and it's as much as we can do to meet each other's eyes. Matthew Forsyth, one of my favourite directors, said once, 'Nicky's the sort of person who ought always to act with a mask on.'

To return to the Benson School. Going on tour was something quite different from present day touring. Most of the large companies travelled by special train, complete with stage staff, scenery and theatre-baskets. Digs were plentiful and, for the most part, excellent, despite the occasional rush for a tin of Keating's Flea Powder. Landladies did all your shopping, provided splendid fires and hot meals after the show. Blankets weren't always adequate—I remember supplementing them with newspapers once or twice. Four or five of us would share a sitting room and the weekly bill would work out at about twelve and six a head.

Some weeks before the Stratford Festival we generally did a season at the Coronet Theatre in Notting Hill Gate. Now it's a cinema but in those days it was quite an important date. Critics from the London Dailies attended our first nights and I considered I was playing in the West End. One night Murray Carrington, who played Oberon, took me in front of the curtain to take a call and I felt once more that I'd arrived. I loved playing Puck, but really I disapprove of boy-parts being played by girls. In these days it happens no longer with the exception of Peter Pan and of course Principal Boys in pantomime. Whenever we played *The Dream*, half-a-dozen local children—a different lot each week—were engaged to make up the requisite number of walk-on fairies. We students were of course called to rehearse on Monday afternoons, which we resented deeply. The rehearsals were conducted by the assistant stage-manager, Pat Nicholson (Irish, but no relation) and I'm sure she hated these extras as much as we did. Their accents varied from week to week, but their personalities seemed identical: noses given to running, and talent practically nil.

Our weeks at the Coronet were delicious. None of us had any money but then nothing cost very much. Even our occasional meals at Soho restaurants didn't set us back more than a few shillings and splendid meals they were. A visit to the cinema cost us sixpence.

Of all my friends in the Benson Company, the two closest were Susan Richmond and Constance Pelissier, who married George Hannam-Clark, nicknamed Cloggie, another staunch Bensonian. I have the happiest memories of Constance, both on tour and at her Golders Green home when I shared her bedroom which we knew affectionately as our 'combined'. One Christmas Constance took me to lunch with her uncle, Harry Pelissier, and there I met his young wife, Fay Compton, and their baby son, Antony, now himself a film director.

My student days were great fun, but as far as work was concerned there never was a young actress of less application than I. Perhaps my Irish blood was responsible for any talent I might have possessed; I'm sure it accounted for my bone-laziness. I enjoyed the making-up and walking-on and was as covetous as anyone of the extra bit of business but as for study, well study meant work. You see, I thought I could act and hadn't begun to realise that acting and work are inseparables. Life on tour was so engrossing. I was for ever falling in and out of love, one day on the point of suicide, the next soaring up to the Seventh Heaven. These occupations didn't mix comfortably with study. On one occasion as I made a flourishing exit, the stage manager remarked, 'I suppose you think you're bloody good.' I suppose I did.

Mr Benson had a habit of sending for you at some inconvenient hour of the morning and expecting you to be prepared with a 'scene'. Very rarely was I prepared. One grim February day at some nine a.m. I arrived at his rooms and found him at breakfast. In this discouraging atmosphere I gave him the benefit of my Prince Arthur. He buttered a piece of toast, bit into it and remarked, 'I don't know. I'm not sure you haven't merely a literary appreciation of the drama.' I left him to finish his toast. I wonder how it was that I didn't there and then give up all ideas of becoming an actress and betake myself to scribbling, always my second string. But I'm afraid, in spite of Mr Benson, I still thought I was 'bloody good'.

From time to time during the tours we students put on shows—always at an uninspiring hour of the morning—watched by Mr Benson and those of the Company who could be persuaded to rise so betimes, and of course any students who were not performing. The principals were always kind and encouraging. Our candid and often scathing critics were our colleagues. To my intense surprise and I imagine Mr Benson's also, I made a hit in a comedy part and soon afterwards became the dazed recipient of my first contract. I think my matinee money stood at one and eightpence: you can work out my weekly salary. But at least it was a salary.

You Never Can Tell was put on at the Stratford Festival for a few performances and I was cast for the part of Dolly. Rehearsals were an ordeal and tears never far away. One night my wretchedness emboldened me to go to Mr Benson's dressing-room. 'I can't do anything if you shout at me,' I blurted out. Greatly daring and I suppose rather impertinent, but the appeal must have borne fruit because he never shouted at me again. But having at last begun to take my work seriously, I realised how vulnerable I was and no longer looked upon acting as fun. Even now I sometimes wonder whether I didn't make the big mistake of my life in going on the stage, but sixty years have leapt by and I'm still at it and better equipped to cope with all it entails of hope and despair.

On the first night of *You Never Can Tell*, when the curtain rose upon me sitting in the dentist's chair, the rehearsals, having to face the Company with Mr Benson demanding, 'Breath, breath, breath:' and myself gulping back tears, were all forgotten. I was on the stage, a professional actress. Somehow or other I made a success. I had some good notices and was convinced that my name was made, only to discover in the next few years that it was nothing of the sort. But for the time being everything was wonderful. I was given a new contract, involving a slight rise in salary, and most of the boy-parts for which, owing to my lack of height, I was supposed to be suited. Not for me the glories of Rosalind or Cleopatra. But though Dolly was my first important part, I made my actual first professional appearance as the Prince of Wales in Richard III. We had rehearsed perfunctorily at the Black Swan, a small inn opposite the theatre, without any 'props' or helpful accessories, simply the bare rehearsal room. When the first night came I found myself confronted with a throne and several steps; there were also royal robes to contend with, and I don't remember even being tried on for them! This would never happen nowadays. The Black Swan, by the way, is now a modernised pub. The old rehearsal room exists no longer, but the pub is still frequented by the Shakespeare Company. It is affectionately known as the 'Dirty Duck'. The name was given it by H.O. and the other day I claimed a bonus from the landlord and received a resplendent ash tray together with nine new pence. Among the features of the Festivals was Spencer, a stage-struck chemist, who took countless photographs of the company in various characters, in a secluded corner of the Memorial garden. The photographs were on display in his shop in the High Street, and did a first-rate trade among theatre fans.

Of all the towns we visited, the high spot was Liverpool, regarded as a sort of Lesser London. A week or two before my first visit there, the young actor to whom I had been unofficially engaged approached me saying 'Look here, you can't go to Liverpool and play the Boy as you're doing now.' And he proceeded to take me through the part. Mr Benson himself couldn't have been more thorough or less complimentary. 'And you ought to get a round on your exit,' he pronounced finally. In those days rounds of applause after an exit were considered an asset.

We opened the week with *Henry the Fifth* and he stood in the wings to watch. I was more nervous than on any first night I've experienced since. But I did get my round and the cautious approval of my teacher. I wonder whether young actors of today would go to such trouble. Perhaps they are too intent on their own performance.

But just about then a cloud blotted out my personal happiness. Gradually we became completely estranged, and I thought I'd never be happy again. How perfectly

Shakespeare understood every facet of the human heart: 'Oh, miserable most, to love unloved!' I could bear that out all right. But youth, thank God, is resilient, and although the scar took a long while to heal, time eventually did its proverbial good work and left me more or less heartwhole.

Playing Shakespearean boys was useful experience enough, but I did long to try something more romantic, and one day an opportunity came my way. Besides the Number One Company there were two others, the North and the South. We were playing at Cardiff when the management received an SOS from the South Company, that week at the Kemble Theatre, Hereford. Their leading lady had been taken ill and there was nobody to play Juliet that night. Could the Number One oblige? The Number One likewise had nobody available. I approached Randle Ayrton, our stage-manager (later to be the best King Lear I've ever seen). Couldn't *I* go? I had played Juliet at school and knew it backwards. Also I'd had the advantage of learning the Benson 'business' as Mr Benson had nobly lent me his prompt-book. 'It won't do you the slightest good—nobody goes to the theatre at Hereford,' said Randle. That didn't matter to me. I would gladly have played in a stable to an audience of cattle so long as I could play Juliet as a professional. Randle gave his grudging consent and off I went. On the journey I swotted my lines and knew I was word perfect. It was a Bank Holiday and the train was late. At Hereford station I was met by a distraught business-manager. They had transferred a scene; there was just time for me to dress and go on for my first entrance. He bustled me into a taxi and in five minutes I was at the theatre, making myself up while someone fastened my dress and did my hair. No time for nerves. Another five minutes and I was on the stage, speaking my first line: 'How now, who calls?'

My Romeo was none other than Henry Baynton, very

beautiful and romantic. He and the rest of the cast were wonderful to me and I must admit I enjoyed every minute. I don't know what sort of performance I gave but at any rate I came through without a dry. Perhaps the ghost of Sarah Siddons, remembering her own days at the Kemble Theatre, came to my aid.

I left the theatre in a daze of happiness. They had fixed me up in a 'combined room' where I spent a sleepless night in the intimate society of a battalion of hungry fleas. But I didn't care. I had played Juliet and however often I might play it again there could never be another performance to touch this.

The next morning I was all set to return to Cardiff. But another crisis had arisen. The leading lady was still absent and there was nobody to take her place that night as Desdemona. 'Oh, couldn't I stay?' I begged. I had never played Desdemona, even at school. All I knew of the play was from a walking-on standpoint. It was madness to attempt it at eight hours' notice. But the management was desperate and a telegram was sent to Cardiff.

For the rest of the day I drove lines into my head and went on at night having memorised perhaps one third of them. The performance was like one of those professional nightmares we all suffer from. The stage-manager sat under my deathbed and gave me the scene line by line. I never thought I should welcome smothering as a consummation devoutly to be wished. The management, no doubt grateful at being delivered from a dilemma, however inadequately, thanked me and sent me back to Cardiff where I received a chilly welcome. Randle Ayrton was furious both with me and the South Company and I walked on in that night's play, properly humbled. My remuneration for the Hereford adventure amounted to one pound. Nothing resulted from it all, but I felt it had been well worth while.

Then came the summer season at Stratford; my last with the Company. I took part in a hilarious burlesque, written by Cloggie—a sort of send-up of *If I Were King*, one of our current productions. I enjoyed the distinction of being the only female member of the Company to be in it, and played a variety of parts ranging from an old man to an impersonation of Justin Huntley Macarthy himself. I'm afraid the author of *If I Were King* wouldn't have found it flattering or even remotely like him. We played to a very select audience and gave only two performances, one of which was graced by the presence of Mr Benson. When he congratulated me on my performance I fancied myself a potential comedy star. My ambition soared when Baliol Holloway labelled me as 'A second Gwennie Mars', at that time the leading comedienne with *The Follies*. I saw myself as her natural successor. Alas for youthful hopes!

The Company was planning an American tour in the coming autumn and we were all approached. The prospect of seeing a new continent was alluring but my ideas about salary didn't fall in with those of the management and my name wasn't included. So the summer season finished. I said goodbye to the precious friends who would soon be bound for the United States, and prepared to face the world of the theatre on my own.

But though I'd left behind me, together with the glamour and the shelter of my first job, some magic I could never recapture, I had brought something away. If I had not yet learnt how to act I had at least learnt how to breathe! And I'd been taught other lessons, however imperfectly learned: patience, humility, and best of all, that something that Old Bensonians like to feel they have derived from their great Chief. I think it's called the Benson Spirit.

IV

GREAT CHARACTERS

My mother and Elaine were in New Zealand for nearly two years. When they returned they had no settled home for some time so I stayed on in Golders Green with the Pelissiers. I spent a good deal of unprofitable time toiling up and down the stairs of agent's offices. Sometimes you'd get an interview with the prospect of work that only too often didn't materialise. Sometimes the interview would end with a curt 'Leave your telephone number.' There was one agent, approached up a frightening little spiral stairway, whose customary greeting was 'No news today.' These encounters were terribly discouraging, but at last I was able to land the part of Essie in *The Devil's Disciple* with Milton Rosmer, who was running a season at Leeds. I was engaged for one week, housed in one of those eternal 'combined rooms', infested with fleas, the inheritance from a Wild West visiting company the previous week. But when you are young even fleas are incapable of daunting you. The door of my room wouldn't stay closed and, when the stage-manager with whom I'd made friends, came to tea, I was obliged to bolt us in. If my landlady had appeared I should certainly have been evicted.

Milton Rosmer wasn't the least alarming, but his wife, Irene Rooke, inspired me with admiration and awe. At an early rehearsal, faced with the ordeal of emitting a piercing scream, I balked at the fence and murmured, 'I can't.' Irene fixed me with a compelling eye. 'But you must,' she said. And of course I did. In the afternoons I used to walk about Roundhay Park practising that scream until I terrified both myself and anyone passing by, and arrived eventually at something approximating to the real thing. At the end of the week I received my salary of three pounds, my first bouquet and a note of congratulations. Once more I felt I had arrived.

Back to Golders Green and more weeks of unemployment. In the spring I went on tour as the ingenue in a play called *Interlopers*. I had to provide my own dress which set me back by at least one week's salary. We all got on very well and shared our general impecunious state with cheerfulness. I remember wandering round Clacton with our leading man in a vain search for a pawnshop.

The Interlopers folded after a few weeks, but one of the company had heard me sing and procured me a job in a Concert Party, *Les Rouges et Noires*, for the summer season at Folkestone. I was engaged to supply light comedy numbers. It was a strange experience for a young actress reared in the Classics. My colleagues were friendly enough, in particular the rather amorous Welsh pianist, but they spoke a jargon new to me. They had absolutely no straight stage experience and found me odd, as undoubtedly I was. We did two shows a day and my weekly salary was two pounds. My singing voice, strong enough for a concert hall, didn't stand up to the open air. One night, while in full song, I spotted my manager halfway down the auditorium, his hand cupped to his ear. That finished me. I invented a pressing interview in London and received my notice to the satisfaction of both artist and manager.

While still at Folkestone, on my way to rehearsal one June morning, I'd read in the newspaper of the assassination of an Austrian Archduke by some Serbian patriots. Tragic, of course, but of less importance to me than the prospect of finding another job. In the heat of those July days I wilted in and out of offices, while rumours of impending war seemed to increase the humid atmosphere.

And then it happened: the First World War. After the feverish excitement had died down, a national reaction that, in these days, strikes one as completely insensitive, dreary days set in. Everyone predicted that the theatres would close but they remained open, often with matinees taking the place of evening performances. Then the long casualty lists began to appear. There was the legendary Retreat from Mons. War became a tragic reality, and though there was still a certain amount of childish flag-waving, despondency enveloped us. 'It will all be over by Christmas' was a slogan no longer.

By this time I had left the shelter of Golders Green and resorted once more to a 'combined' in a house kept by a cheerful Cockney landlady with whom I formed a lasting friendship. A minute film part came my way. I don't remember the name of the film or the director, but the studio was located somewhere in Bayswater, within walking distance of my room in Elgin Crescent. I got three days work at the daily rate of a pound and, feeling very prosperous, bought myself a second-hand fur coat. The film was of course a 'Silent'; talkies were more than ten years distant.

Then, through a chance meeting with an Old Bensonian, I heard that a Shakespearean season had started at the Victoria Hall in the Waterloo Road, with a production of *The Tempest*, opening shortly. Down I went with a repertoire of songs and suffered an audition for Ariel and somehow or other I was offered the part. I can't remember my interview with Lilian Baylis and I still wonder how I got it. Perhaps the fact that I came of a clerical family had some influence, for Miss Baylis was a devout Anglican. Ben Greet was our director (producer in those days) a dear, white-haired tyrant whom I loved and hated in equal proportions. He and I crossed swords on several occasions. One night, during the last scene of the *Dream*, I overheard him in the wings grumbling about the green drapery I was wearing as Titania, which I considered lovely, but he thought spoiled the dazzling whiteness of the scene. I walked off the stage and we bandied fierce words. I returned to the stage, humbled but at peace with my assailant, and continued to sport the green drapery.

Then a real peace, an exciting sort of peace, descended on us with the arrival of Sybil Thorndike. She advanced upon us on a flood-tide of exuberance, good-will, good-nature and above all, sheer goodness. A star danced and there she was. Fifty odd years ago but time has dealt so beautifully with her that for me and I think for every-one, she is the same radiant person now, when she is ninety. She and I shared an apology for a dressing-room where we chatted and joked and jostled each other as we dressed elbow to elbow. I can still hear her saying, 'Don't be a fool, Nick!' as doubtless she would today if the occasion should arise.

From time to time Lewis Casson, home on leave, would look in at a rehearsal. I was a little afraid of the solemn gentleman in sergeant's uniform. I felt he might endorse Sybil's 'Don't be a fool' and probably more forcibly. I had already encountered him once or twice. Our first meeting had been in his dressing-room at the Coronet Theatre during one of Miss Horniman's London seasons. I'd only just left the Benson Company and didn't know how to behave at an interview. Lewis surveyed me from beneath his formidable brows, suffered my halting sentences for a while and then said, 'Don't keep raising your eyebrows, it kills your face.' The mobile eyebrows went up another half-inch. 'I don't do it on purpose—it just happens,' I replied. I'd endured this sort of criticism from my mother from my youth up: 'gutters' she used to call the horizontal lines on my fore-head. No doubt they did kill my face. By now it must be stone-dead, though it doesn't worry me any more.

I made my second attack on Lewis later on, my first having borne no fruit. He was staying in St George's Square, the home of Sybil's father, Canon Thorndike. I don't remember much of that interview except that on making my exit I said timidly, 'May I write to you again, Mr Casson?' 'Oh yes,' said he amiably, 'I have a large wastepaper basket.' Fortunately I possessed a glimmer of humour and the statement amused me instead of sending me away in tears. In later years, when Lewis had become one of my dearest friends and had directed me in many plays, I used to remind him of those sallies which he'd forgotten and emphatically denied.

But if, in those far off days, Lewis was formidable, Sybil was the exact opposite. She was universally friendly; everyone adored her. We played three times a week at the Vic, the other nights being devoted to opera. Our salaries were ten shillings a show. I think Sybil got fifteen as she played most of the leads. What enchanting shows she gave! One of her best was Lady Macbeth— probably her finest performance. I remember saying to her, 'Oh, you are a great actress!' Was I the first to say that, I wonder?

My six months at the Vic passed in a welter of hard work, vaulting ambition, romance of course, and a certain amount of privation. My salary, eked out by help from home, didn't allow of riotous living. We used to lunch at an adjacent Express Dairy, long since demolished. The menu was usually sausage-and-mash and coffee, costing about one and threepence. We gossiped incessantly and I forgot my headmistress's warning and ridiculed all and sundry, but good-humouredly, I hope. Andrew Leigh of blessed memory was stage-manager, J. Leslie Frith one of my great chums, and of course Sybil and I were the closest of friends. One day, walking down the Waterloo Road, she said, 'Nick, I believe I'm going to have another baby.' This turned out to be Ann, who as time went on, became another dear friend and a fine actress.

I played a variety of parts: Titania, Jessica, Mopsa in *The Winter's Tale* (in which Dorothy Ilma, William Stack and I sang a love-lorn trio) and the Courtesan in *A Comedy of Errors*. Ben Greet, with Puritan reticence, re-named her 'Phryne'. Rehearsals were long but never too long, we enjoyed them so much. I think we did a fresh play every week and I was in most of them.

At my digs, boiled eggs were my staple diet, but I

m anaged to thrive and even went so far as to start on a
novel, never finished. Its skeleton, poor thing, still
exists, hidden away in some cupboard. I think the hero
was based on Baliol Holloway, for whom, in common
with most young women of his acquaintance, I maintained something of a hero-worship. Later on I came to
know him and his wife, Emil, intimately, and hero-
worship diminished as friendship grew. We used to
reminisce about old Benson days and I never tired of
hearing him talk of his early years in the theatre. His
friends were for ever begging him to write his autobiography, but humble man that he was, he insisted that
nobody would be interested. And here am I, so far
behind him in talent and reputation, daring to attempt
my own.

As we were playing only three performances a week at
the Vic, I was able to see other plays in the West End.
In those days the pit cost half-a-crown, gallery a shilling,
so even on my modest resources I could go fairly often.
Gerald du Maurier, Lewis Waller, Beerbohm Tree,
the Bourchiers, Marie Löhr, Madge Titheradge, to
mention only a few, were all at the height of their
careers. And of course Gladys Cooper, perhaps the most
celebrated of them all. In my student days I had seen
Milestones, in which she and Owen Nares played the
juveniles. There never was a more enchanting couple.
All this play-going should have given me some fine
lessons in acting, and although I don't think I profited
greatly, I certainly saw myself as one of their number at
some future date.

In the early autumn of 1915 I embarked on a job that
began auspiciously and finished in disillusionment.
Consuelo de Reyes, a schoolmate of mine at Leamington,
was running a Soldiers' Club, and another club for
girls, together with all kinds of social activities in an
eighteenth-century house she rented in Bath, called
Citizen House. She asked me to come down to run the

Soldiers' Club, but when I got there I found myself requisitioned for a multitude of other duties. Chief among them was to produce plays for the club girls. They were written by Miss de Reyes herself and were remarkable pieces of work. (I believe they could be revived even now; their psychology was far ahead of the time.) Lola, as Miss de Reyes was called, was a dynamic personality. She ruled over the house and its activities and expected everyone to be as tireless as herself. Miss Hope, her self-effacing partner, and Lola herself, were rich and ran the place on such luxurious lines that I used to feel a bit ashamed of my beautiful room and the lavish food. My salary, by war-time standards, was princely. Every kind of 'prop' or material I required for the plays were provided without the slightest demur. Had it not been for the soldiers who crowded into the big concert hall for their weekly concerts, you would scarcely have known there was a war on.

Lola had absolutely no sense of time. There were no set hours for work, and the work was exhausting, but at first I loved it all. The plays were absorbing and the girls enthusiastic; the Soldiers' Club, where we sang jolly patriotic songs such as 'Pack Up Your Troubles', kept them all happy. It was surprising how the soldiers, inclined to ribaldry, would respond to the more serious numbers I thought necessary to insert from time to time.

Then gradually things began to change. It couldn't have been jealousy, Lola was far too talented herself for that, but somehow as time went on she took 'agin' me and life at Citizen House became unbearable. She would insinuate her own ideas into my productions. I may not have been very experienced but the theatre was my job and I resented interference. When at last I collected enough courage to give in my notice, she was probably as glad to be rid of me as I was to go. The train that bore me down to Cornwall on a visit to Constance and her husband, Geoffrey Silver, a naval officer stationed at Plymouth, disgorged an emaciated, nerve-wracked and completely exhausted person. In the society of the Silvers and their young family I picked up soon enough. One day Geoffrey brought the news that a friend of his, a Mr King of the Plymouth Repertory Theatre, was looking for an actress to play Mrs Arbuthnot in *A Woman of No Importance*, and Geoffrey had suggested me. Of course I jumped at the chance. I was years too young for the part, but reinforced by a grey wig and my mother's dresses, somehow or other I got by without disaster. The part was interminably long and we had only one week to rehearse. I'd no difficulty in learning the lines: it was the part itself that daunted me. Written in Oscar Wilde's most artificial style, the characters expressed themselves almost exclusively in epigrams, and conveyed no semblance of real life. Especially the unfortunate Mrs Arbuthnot. Lord Illingworth, her partner in what was considered an unforgivable past, was played by Frederick Victor. In the last act I reached high drama by slapping him smartly on the cheek with his glove. Our next encounter on the stage, many years later, was in *Six Men of Dorset*—a beautiful contrast to *A Woman of No Importance*. By a coincidence I was again the wrong age for my part, but this time about a generation too old. I shall talk about that later on.

By now my mother had taken a flat in St John's Wood, and there she, Elaine and I spent the remaining years of the war. The days of servants being past, we were waited on by a succession of elusive 'dailies'. During their frequent absences I learnt cooking and housework the hard way. Most of the household duties fell to me as Elaine was away all day at the Censorship. At first she dealt mainly with French and German, but later on she made a daring onslaught on the three Scandinavian languages. Perhaps her early years in Sweden had left a subconscious aptitude for these unpronounceable tongues.

While in St John's Wood we came in for a good many air raids: major calamities that faded into insignificance when compared with those of twenty-five years later.

One raid came perilously near us when the Princess of Wales Public House in Abbey Road was hit.

I played my first character part in the summer of 1916. The play was an egregious melodrama entitled *The Dawn of Happiness*, produced at Dalston and the small girl who played a leading part was billed as 'Little Angela Baddeley'. Having done mostly Shakespeare and a few modern plays, I was almost as thrown by their theatrical habits as I had been by those of *Les Rouges et Noires*. My colleagues consumed glasses of port during the performance and spoke in a parlance strange to my young ears. The play itself was beyond belief: a railway accident in which the heroine, like Rapunzel, let down her hair, a bearded villain, and a leading man who sang 'You'll remember me' in a mellifluous tenor voice. We lived through one week of this and then *The Dawn of Happiness* faded into everlasting night.

I don't know how it came about, but a little later on I was sent for by Fred Terry to audition for Julia Neilson's understudy in *Sweet Nell of Old Drury*. A notable piece of miscasting, my five foot two pitted against Julia's regal stature, but she invariably chose a small girl for her Sweet Nell understudy. I spent hours on Hampstead Heath studying the part, and when the day came I went to the New Theatre to be confronted by Mr and Mrs Terry, looming large and alarming. I really had no idea of how the part should be played, and just went for it baldheaded. Fred was delightfully genial; Julia, swathed in trailing furs and scarves in defiance of the broiling July day, was gracious in her own absent-minded way, and the result was that I was engaged for the autumn tour at a salary of four pounds a week, which I thought quite magnificent considering the comparatively light work expected of me.

I stayed with the Terrys for nearly two years. Our repertoire consisted of *Sweet Nell* and *The Scarlet Pimpernel*. Besides being understudy, I walked on in both plays. Also I used to be deputed, on the nights when Julia didn't feel her voice was up to standard, to sing the Orange Cries which preceded her first entrance as Sweet Nell. Something of an ordeal, matching my voice with hers. In the *Pimpernel* her understudy had a harder task. Sometimes she had to sing 'Eldorado' at the side of the stage, while Julia, her back to the audience, stood by the harpsichord and made-believe. For one horrific week, when the understudy was away with mumps, I was roped in to take her place. Far more alarming than the Orange Cries.

Julia, though in her middle forties, was still the most beautiful woman I had ever seen, but her acting wasn't in the same class as her looks. Fred, as Sir Percy Blakeney and Charles II, gave impeccable performances—flamboyant, larger than life—in keeping with the period and the style of acting in those days. When, a few years later, I saw *The Pimpernel* from the stalls, I realised how artificial that type of acting was. But Fred Terry was a master in his own line. When not suffering from his frequent attacks of gout he could be a superb director, though his outbursts of fury could be frightening. Once or twice he would take an understudy rehearsal and many's the time that I nearly bit holes in my cheeks to keep back the tears which would certainly have increased his fury. Sometimes, following one of my most heinous breaches of technique, he would murmur reproachfully, 'And you a Bensonian!' Then, after storming at you for half-an-hour, he would say, with the legendary Terry smile, 'I only ask for a little intelligence, m'dear.'

We played mostly in the north of England with occasional visits to Scotland. Blackburn, Halifax and Sunderland were depressing dates in wartime. My first winter with the Terrys was especially cold. 'Combined rooms' were a luxury as you could be sure of a fire to see you to bed. The price of rations was considered extortionate—butter at half-a-crown a pound, a rare luxury. But in many ways the war made no special impact on our lives, except for our own private anxieties.

However, we did come in for a few Zeppelin raids. One night at Nottingham we had one during the show. The audience, at the request of Fred, remained seated, while those of us not on the stage stood in the wings, holding lighted candles to enliven the performers while Fred and Julia went imperturbably through their last scene.

Except in the theatre itself we didn't see much of our two chiefs, but sometimes they gave luncheon-parties, ceremonious affairs with Julia sitting silent at the head of the table. Occasionally you would come across them in the street, walking slowly, rather as though heading a procession. Once, I remember coming upon them standing in the middle of the pavement, tearing up envelopes and tossing the pieces nonchalantly into the gutter. They really were Royal Personages.

One of the girls in the company professed to tell fortunes. She read my hand and predicted great success in the future. Of course I took that to mean in the next few years or even months. I can laugh now at my youthful credulity but at the time it wasn't so funny and I felt a deep sense of disappointment as the years went by.

In those days I was a compulsive visitor to fortune-tellers. My sister Angela and I, during a period of depression, would say, 'We're fit to go to a seer' and off we would go. These individuals were usually located in an up-stairs room in Edgware Road or one of the suburbs. As a rule the fee was about half-a-crown; on rare occas-ions we'd spring to ten shillings. The wealthy marriages, the four children, the fabulous success in the theatre—they all loomed large on the palm or in the cards. Perhaps my being left-handed was a handicap—the seers must be forgiven if they made somewhat contradictory pre-dictions. In the States, where fortunetellers abounded, I lost interest, or maybe gained a little common-sense.

By the end of 1917 I felt due for a change, so I bade the Terrys a fond goodbye and set out once more to try my luck in London. A bad bit of timing: I was out of work for the rest of the winter.

tterings at the piano didn't matter. He could still
ke magic music. I so well recall his coming on to the
tform and carefully dusting the piano-stool before
ing down to play. At Christmas there was the panto-
me at the Hippodrome, scarcely a high-class enter-
ment. One of the more topical jokes: 'Up with the
k and to bed with the Wrens' caused some embar-
ment to ourselves and our male escorts.

light duty was something of a respite. We worked
n eight o'clock until two next morning with a brief
od of sleep in an evil-smelling little shed containing
beds and the society of mice which had an awful
ct on me. There were never more than two of us on
y at night. With Miss Hamblen safe at home, Rob
I used to bring in our mattresses, brew cocoa, sleep
rmittently and carry on telephone conversations
our opposite numbers at other stations. Out of these
ight talks arose many a small romance. The ratings
he US Naval Base would ring up, saying mourn-
, 'Ma'am, I'm lonely,' and long conversations would
e. As the war drew to an end our nights were fairly
from official calls and messages so we had quite a
ant time. One of my special boy-friends was a
alist which of course endeared him to me. We used
eet whenever possible and partake of severely-
ned meals. It was all very innocent and consoling.

wish I had a photograph of the Wrens in the First
d War: hideous blue serge uniforms, topped by
coming overcoats and horrid little caps. During the
d war I sometimes encountered delightfully equip-
young ladies and would inquire tentatively how
enjoyed being in the Wrens. 'Super!' came the
able reply.

mother and Elaine relieved my monotonous life
ying me a short visit, which was bliss, and on one
id occasion Geoffrey Silver took me out to dinner
oused much comment from the girls. 'Fancy Nick
out with a Commander!' I'm sure Geoffrey

V

CHAMELEON'S DISH

1918 was a gloomy winter. The war dragged on and looked like going for ever, with heavy losses and nothing to lift the general depression. To enliven my enforced leisure, Angela and I wrote a novel together. The agent to whom we sent it was favourably impressed but declared it unsuitable for publication as it was in letter form, not a popular one. Encouraged by the agent's reaction, I ought perhaps to have carried on writing, but I was easily daunted and let time slip by without doing anything. I was restless and despondent, feeling I was making no advance in any direction. I did a few abortive bits of war-work, and at last, instead of trying to impress upon my boy-friends the necessity of joining up, decided that it was about time I did some real service myself. So I applied for a post in the WRNS. I put in for a telephonist's job. If I'd known what it entailed I would have chosen something else. I was all against trying for a commission, feeling I'd enough to do looking after myself without supervising a team of other girls.

The necessary preliminaries having been accomplished, I sat down to await my call-up. It came towards the end of July. I was to proceed to a hostel in Courtfield Gardens and start my training. I shall never forget that first evening. On arrival I was conducted upstairs and subjected to a vigorous shampoo although I protested that I'd washed my hair the night before. Furthermore, my head was ruthlessly attacked by a toothcomb. I was then allotted a bed in a dormitory with eight other trainees. This was an invasion I thought I'd never get used to, but after a few nights I settled down.

While awaiting our training course, I and my co-telephonists were put on to stewarding, which meant washing-up for about a hundred and fifty souls, and scrubbing floors and tables. At first our feet ached so excruciatingly that we were unable to sleep. I would sit up, trying to read by the light of the moon streaming in through the uncurtained windows. But it was surprising how quickly our aching feet grew acclimatised.

My mates were mostly a jolly, friendly lot, and time passed pleasantly enough. We were allowed one afternoon off per week. I used to go home and bask briefly in what I called civilisation. Then the day dawned when we were ordered to proceed to London Wall Telephone Exchange, and life took on a new turn. I suppose our supervisors were efficient teachers but they were tremendously strict and seemed to demand perfection almost before we had mastered the intricacies of the switchboard. We were transferred later to Admiralty Trunks for further training. After unloading from the bus at Charing Cross, we marched down Whitehall, and I was given the proud responsibility of leading our band of about half-a-dozen ratings. It delighted my sense of the dramatic to encounter an officer and call out, 'Eyes right!'; only more often than not I'd forget to give the counter-command and left my friends to continue their march with heads craning anxiously at nothing.

Our training at the Admiralty was pretty gruelling. I can't say I enjoyed any of it but at last it was over and I was posted. My destination was the Private Branch Exchange at Mount Wise, Devonport. I was billeted in Plymouth at a small house in North Road, kept by Miss Jones, a minute person with a soft Devonshire voice but quite an authoritative way with her. There were six of us telephonists. I shared a bedroom with two of them: Flack, a flamboyant red-head, and Robinson, a bright irreverent Cockney, rather like a cat with her shaggy black hair and huge grey eyes. Eventually she and I became great friends and for years afterwards we kept up with each other. At first I regarded my companions somewhat snobbishly, but I was soon cured of that. Robinson, a raconteur of racy stories, used to delight in

imitating my exclamations of 'Disgusti... was pleased to call my Kensington acce...

Our bedroom provided only one w... three of us. Flack and Rob were ... sketchiest of ablutions and would ca... Nick washing herself!', while I attempt... cleanliness. We all enjoyed a weekly s... baths, however.

We took our meals with Miss Jone... kitchen and fed frugally, chiefly on b... stew and sausages. Butter was a luxu... for tea which we took with us to t... Wise was a lonely little place. The si... switchboard and message-room wh... signals. One or two ancient naval m... storey. What their duties were re... they were known to us as 'Topsides'.

My first few weeks at Mount Wis... We were supervised by a Wren Offi... At first she nearly drove me crazy, ... back and calling out, 'Quick, Nic... plugged into the wrong number w... always. I remember cutting off no... mander-in-Chief in the middle of ar... tion and being reduced to ignon... heart Miss Hamblen was quite a ... me out rations of her own china te... brew prepared by Miss Jones, an... became quite fond of her. After... sometimes met her again and ... Devonport miseries.

On our free afternoons Rob an... splendid café called Goodbody's, ... many cakes as rationing allowed ... our very slim pay—I forget the ... run to luxuries. There were very ... At the Guildhall there were occ... mann gave a heavenly Chopin r...

jeopardised his exalted position by consorting in public with a humble rating. Another of our isolated amusements was a dance given at the Guildhall for officers and ratings at the various stations, graced by the presence of Mrs Waldorf Astor, later to become Viscountess Astor. And just before I was demobbed we at Mount Wise gave a gala concert of our own. We performed under my personal direction. (I felt very grand and professional.) I think some of our turns occasioned raised official eyebrows, particularly those of Miss Hamblen.

And at last it was Armistice Day. Eleven o'clock on the eleventh day of the eleventh month. The reiterated number rang out like a carillon of rejoicing. The bruised and torn world was waiting now to have its wounds bound and be made into a world fit for heroes to live in. But today everyone was in the same delirious state as that in which the war had started. We had cast off the grim trappings of war and were entering upon an eternity of peace. Never again, we told ourselves, would homes be broken up, youth give itself away with such heartbreaking readiness. England would settle down and take up life just where she had thrown it away more than four years ago.

That night we Wrens were granted a late pass until half-past ten. My colleagues were all fixed up with their own escorts, none of mine were available so I set out to enjoy a solitary celebration. I was indulging in a poached egg at a café when in burst a couple of young Marines who, seeing me alone, 'picked me up'. We enjoyed our communal meal while they told me about life in their recent billet: the frightful rations, the discipline, the lack of feminine society, a story I'd heard many times before. All too soon it was ten-thirty and Cinderella was due back at her own billet. My two swains saw me home with promises of further meetings, and thus ended my Armistice Day. I wonder how my successors spent their VE Day.

I endured another three months at Mount Wise, but by that time I'd grown accustomed to the routine and telephone calls no longer alarmed me. In February I managed to wangle my discharge on 'personal' grounds. I was free to return to civilian life and the theatre. I arrived home with a small gratuity, bobbed hair and a profound sense of relief. I also contrived to earn thirty shillings from the *Daily Mirror* for an article written in my heart's blood about the experiences of a telephonist in wartime.

Immediately after being demobbed I began to think seriously of giving up the stage and trying my hand at writing. I had a sympathetic mentor in G E Morrison, whom I'd met at Stratford, then dramatic critic on the *Morning Post*, the paper later to be incorporated with the *Daily Telegraph*. But before long I had collected a handful of polite rejection slips and I was back on the stage. It was J B Fagan's *The Merchant of Venice* at the Royal Court Theatre that lured me back. I understudied Edith Evans as Nerissa and walked on as a page. Nerissa was several sizes too small for Edith, but even so, her genius shone through as it does in everything she plays. All through that season we were great friends, and though we don't often meet nowadays I retain a warm affection for her; not the easy relationship I have with Sybil; there is something a bit royal about Edith. I met it in Frank Benson and Fred Terry; they always seemed to be wearing crowns, whereas Sybil's head is bare of anything—except perhaps a halo.

The Russian actor, Maurice Moscovitsch, was the Shylock, a magnificent performance. Fagan's wife, Mary Grey, played Portia. Beautiful and statuesque, she was a size too big for the part. Mrs Patrick Campbell after watching a performance, is reputed to have remarked, 'My dear, you were *great!*'

During the run of *The Merchant* I played in a season of Christmas Matinees at the St Martin's Theatre. The play was *Once Upon a Time*, and I was a young person of extreme ugliness, named Fishface, which I doubled with the part of a little old man, silent but active; I enjoyed both, but especially the old man. Also in the cast was Margaret Scudamore, scion of a theatrical family. We became very friendly, and I remember going to her house in Belgravia where I made the acquaintance of her schoolboy son, Michael. My chief memory of him is that he was a brilliant pianist. I didn't meet him again for many years, when he was the famous Sir Michael Redgrave.

The forceful Edie Craig, Ellen Terry's daughter, directed *Once Upon a Time*. I loved working with her and didn't find her the least formidable. She had none of her mother's radiant beauty but a great deal of her charm. Her methods were decided, and of course, like all the Terrys, she was a perfectionist.

J B Fagan released me from *The Merchant* to go into a new production, sponsored by my old friend, Hubert Woodward. I think he was the first agent with whom I ever had dealings. He gave me lots of jobs, always for the lowest possible pay. He is still hale and hearty and carrying on indefatigably. He still offers me an occasional job, and I'm happy to say the rate of pay has increased with the years. This particular play was *The Fold*, by the late Marchioness Townshend, about suburban infidelity. Godfrey Tearle and Hilda Trevelyan played husband and wife. Hilda was a dear little compact person with a matter-of-fact manner, beneath which blossomed a fund of humour, pathos and a wonderful sense of the theatre. Godfrey was perhaps more of a personality than a great actor. I remember his remarking that his wife always said that his popularity as an actor was sustained by his looks rather than his acting ability. But as the years went by, he achieved many successes in the theatre, notably Othello at Stratford and Hamlet in the West End.

Prominent in the cast was Mrs A B Tapping, a name forgotten by anyone at the present day, but in her time a veteran actress of a school which even then was beginning to be dated. If we considered her 'ham' then to the present generation she'd be a 'super ham'. Although in appearance a bit alarming, with her massive presence and sombre brown eyes, she was really loveable. A little disconcerting to act with as she had a distressing cough, apt to interfere with your best lines. This was doubtless due to incessant smoking. On tour we lived in the same house, and I would look in on her to say good-night, to find her, supper at an end, sitting very upright at the table, cigarette-ash spilling from her ample bosom on to the tablecloth and beside her a tumbler in which reposed a fine set of teeth. She had bequeathed some of her peculiarities to her daughter, Sydney Fairbrother, a character actress of some repute, with a passion for small animals. Quite often a pet rat could be discerned, nestling among her furs. For that reason alone I'm glad we never met, as I have an obsessional terror of rats and mice. When I encounter a mouse I don't merely jump on a chair—I faint dead away!

Another member of the cast was Holman Clark, much in demand in the twenties as actor and producer. During our London run he was directing *Mary Rose* at the Haymarket, and would give glowing accounts of the young actress, Fay Compton, who according to him 'Never put a foot wrong'—a eulogy she has continued to live up to.

I myself had a really excellent character part, a garrulous spinster named Miss Plum. Once again I imagined I'd reached the turning point in my career. But in spite of good notices it bore me no fruit at the time. Five years after, on the strength of this almost forgotten part, J B Fagan engaged me for Charlotte, the governess in *The Cherry Orchard*.

Our director for *The Fold* was Stanley Drewitt, a former member of Miss Horniman's Company at the Gaiety, Manchester. Now he *was* formidable. At re-

hearsal he would say, 'Miss Nicholson, be more definite!'
(In those days we were all 'Miss' and 'Mister'.) We had a
bumper try-out at Manchester, in that same Gaiety
Theatre, but after a glamorous first night in London at
the Queen's Theatre, we faded out in a few weeks. All
the same, we were booked by David Belasco for a season
in New York, but for some reason it fell through, to our
huge disappointment.

I had a very lean winter. I went down to Woking as a
fill-in, to direct an amateur company in *A Pair of Silk
Stockings*. A delightful young girl was playing the lead.
Here's someone promising, I thought, and sure enough I
was right. For the young girl was Barbara Couper and
I'm proud to have been perhaps the person who encouraged her to go on the stage. It didn't take her long to
make her name both as a broadcaster and in many a
play in the West End. I think it was while at the BBC
that she married Howard Rose, senior drama producer.
I was with her in one or two radio plays and quite lately
she and I played sisters in a television play.

1921 took me on a transatlantic tour of Galsworthy's
Skin Game. I'd been longing to play in the States ever
since our disappointment over *The Fold*, and though the
Company wasn't very distinguished I was thrilled at the
prospect. Starring in the London company was the
unforgettable Meggie Albanesi whose death in her early
twenties robbed us of one of our brightest stars. Galsworthy himself came to a few of our rehearsals and I
met him once or twice: a charming, self-effacing man of
whom one marvelled that he could have created Irene
Forsyte, admired by most men I've met, but nearly
always disliked by her own sex.

It was the longest and hottest summer I can remember.
We sailed off to Canada at the end of August. I nearly
died of seasickness, but at last came the calm of the St
Lawrence river where only a few years ago Irving's son
Laurence and his wife, Mabel Hackney, met their
tragic death. We opened our tour in Montreal. I used to

call it the 'chameleon' city—you'd walk down one street and think you were in France, and then you'd come upon an avenue of trees and you were back in England. The theatre was old and uncomfortable and the dressing-rooms faced a balcony looking straight on to the stage. Visits to the lavatory during a performance were taboo: the sound of plumbing was embarrassingly audible. It was glorious summer weather; we would stroll along the streets, eating peaches. But our meals were frugal and the hotels available to us on our modest salaries were often infested with undesirables such as cockroaches. We moved on to Toronto, which seemed another Manchester, and then began a long spell at small Canadian towns, one night in each, some of them beautiful, standing amid lakes and rivers, others reminding us of the less attractive towns of our own country. Three nights in London, Ontario, seemed like a season after our protracted one-night stands.

We left Canada and embarked on a tour of the States —Detroit, Cleveland and finally a season in Chicago. By this time I was involved in a love-affair, and Chicago —its winds strong with carnivorous whiffs from the adjacent stockyards, its ear-splitting traffic and all—was to me a city of enchantment. This romance of mine spread over many years and for good and ill had a profound influence on my life and outlook. My religious beliefs evaporated and every other interest went by the board under the influence of this overwhelming obsession, for obsession it was. Even being out of work didn't bother me much. I had set up an altar and dedicated it to someone who to me was God and man in one. In those days I did nothing by halves. 'Never put your eggs into one basket' was a maxim I ignored. Long years have taught me many lessons and now any eggs I may possess are nicely distributed.

The work in Chicago was hard going. Sometimes we played ten or eleven shows a week, Sundays included, and by the time our three months' season was over the parts we played had become so familiar as to seem almost meaningless. We went down to New York for a few days' respite, followed by a week playing what is now known as 'Off Broadway'. I hated my first acquaintance with New York: noisy, expensive and so cosmopolitan as to seem de-nationized. I learnt to appreciate it only after my next visit, several years later. By that time my whole outlook on life had changed. I suppose that fundamentally our characters don't alter, but they have so many facets. Perhaps, like Montreal, I'm essentially a chameleon.

It was April when we set sail for England: a long, stormy passage in a cockleshell ship, involving me once again in agonising seasickness for the first few days. The sight of England's green fields and budding trees gave me no thrill. From then onwards I was living in a sort of secret garden, populated by only one person: an Eden in which I persisted in ignoring the presence of a serpent. Later on it overwhelmed me and despair took the place of ecstasy. But once more under the parental roof, I felt the need to get away from its influence. I persuaded my mother to let me go off on my own. After much searching I found a minute dwelling which I glorified by the name of a flat but really it consisted of one large room and a tiny kitchenette in the basement of a house in Doughty Street. My landlord was an eccentric person named Marshall Wood who, though friendly, turned out to be a liability. Through him I became the unwilling participant in a complicated incident involving a nefarious gentleman impersonating a Vine Street policeman. Unfortunately, I happened to be calling on Mr Wood at the same time as this character, and was subpoenaed to appear as a witness in the lawsuit that ensued at the Old Bailey. It was conducted by Sir Ernest Wild, a Cambridge friend of H.O.'s. I don't recall the details but I was acutely nervous, and being called upon to identify the guilty party I met his eye and for some time went in fear that he might seek me out for revenge. Not unnaturally I took a dislike to Doughty Street and began looking for another home. I lit on a small flat in the heart of theatreland. It was splendid to be within walking distance of the theatres. Coming home in the small hours from a protracted dress-rehearsal gave me a feeling of emancipation, though perhaps it wasn't a very suitable milieu for a young actress on her own.

Although the rent of this small flat was absurdly low, and I had constant help from my mother and my immensely generous brother, I seemed always to be in low water. I think my horrible tendency to run up bills was much to blame. I tried ineffectually to deal with them by selling and often pawning such of my possessions that were at all marketable. I had very little jewellery. One or two family portraits (great-uncles whom I'd never known and from their appearances hadn't wanted to know) a few first editions—oh, how much I've regretted them!—and the beautiful christening robe of white satin and Honiton lace presented by my god-mother, came under the hammer. Doubtless I'd made a fine figure at the font, but the robe seemed to be serving a more useful purpose in earning half a guinea to settle an outstanding laundry bill. Later on, the lovely set of amethysts, left me by my mother, likewise shared a gloomy end. I continued these transactions for a good many years. Today, my happier circumstances and perhaps a more sensible attitude to money matters, have delivered me from these necessities.

It was while living in the little West End flat that my godless outlook began to irk me. I found it impossible to live without some sort of anchor. Orthodoxy no longer had any appeal: I looked around for something else to steady my unstable mind. Some of my friends in the theatre were Christian Scientists. I'd never been in the habit of going to doctors, so perhaps the idea of dispensing with them altogether was one reason why I began discussing and eventually studying Mary Baker Eddy's book, *Science and Health with Key to the Scriptures.* I still think there is much to be said for some of its teaching, but gradually I sensed a sort of chill in the impersonal atmosphere of those services I used to attend weekly. Perhaps I missed the ritual to which I'd so long been accustomed; perhaps I felt the need of the priesthood, though even after I had slipped away from Christian Science I was still hovering about in a vague state of unbelief. Was I to taste of the Chameleon's Dish for the rest of my life? Would I never find stability? I was for ever seeking for a settled happiness. Love and friendship would sometimes bring me near to it; work contributed from time to time, but the Chameleon's Dish remained my staple diet.

VI
NEW DEPARTURES AND OLD FRIENDS

In the inter-war years there were many more theatres than there are now. Some have been bombed; some are transformed into cinemas or blocks of offices. One of these was the Regent Theatre in Euston Road. For a short time Nigel Playfair ran a season there. The most notable of the plays was Carel Kapek's *Insect Play*, a Czech masterpiece that never got its deserts here. This was a landmark in my life, not on account of my part in it (I understudied Maire O'Neill and played the minute role of an Ant) but because it was here that I met John Gielgud for the first time. He had only recently left Lady Benson's dramatic school where H.O. and he were master and pupil. John still talks of this, and I know my brother was proud to have helped a little to set him on the road to fame. In *The Insect Play* he was a butterfly, believe it or not: a slim young man of nineteen, rather awkward and gangling, full of promise but a long way from the flowering of the genius that was to give him first place in the heirarchy of the theatre. One of his greatest performances was of *The Ages of Man*, with which he opened the rebuilt Queen's Theatre after it had been practically gutted in the war. I remember rushing round to congratulate him, to which effusion he responded, 'Were you pleased?' What did it matter that *I* was pleased? But that was all part of his unexampled humility. Only the truly great are truly humble.

All through the long years our friendship has never faltered. His mother embodied all the elegance of the Victorian age. I used to visit her at her flat in Queen's Gate, a veritable theatre museum with countless photographs of John who was her idol. I so well recall her funeral, some years ago; all of us in tears, and Mac, John's faithful dresser and friend, his eyes brimming as he murmured, 'I've come without my teeth.' Mac is a legendary figure, having served under Martin Harvey and Fred Terry long before he came to dress John. Now well over eighty he is as lively and efficient as ever. Dressers are a very special breed. They seem to possess an extra sense, anticipating your needs, and never the least perturbed by quick changes and temperamental artists. My favourite of all is Frieda Nerupka. She has dressed me in many productions and is like one of the family. You can confide in her and know your confidence will drop into a well and never be drawn up again.

In the early 1920s I made my first acquaintance with radio. Broadcasting was gradually coming into being. We possessed small wireless sets, many of them home-made, from which a crystal and two mysterious little wires known as cats' whiskers, produced the very varying sound. The most popular programmes were supplied by orchestras, principally the Savoy Orpheans and, of course, Henry Hall and his Band. I went for an audition to Savoy Hill, known as 2LO, and a little later made my first broadcast in Yeats' *Land of Heart's Desire*, under the direction of Howard Rose. An absolute perfectionist, he had the reputation of correcting an inflexion almost before the performer had a chance to make it. I found him stimulating and though he certainly corrected me constantly, I was really grateful. Broadcasting came to be one of my favourite activities; the very fact of reading from a script gives you confidence, and it's a wonderful exercise for voice and diction. Those early broadcasts were primitive affairs compared with the sophisticated programmes at Broadcasting House. All the same they were serious occasions. No casual sweaters and jeans for the men, and on transmission nights evening dress was expected. Of course all performances were 'live' and consequently more of an ordeal than now when nearly everything is recorded.

My own broadcasts in the early days were infrequent. Most of my jobs were in the theatre. I have spoken of *The Cherry Orchard*, which Fagan produced at the little old Royalty Theatre in 1925. Here again I was associated with John Gielgud who was playing Trophimov. James Whale, later to make his name in America, was in the cast, and many other actors now celebrated. Dear Fred O'Donovan was one of them. Later on he transferred himself to television and was noted for using only one camera. My own performance of Charlotte I considered rather good at the time, but when a few years ago I saw the part played by Patience Collier at the Lyric, Hammersmith, I was obliged to change my opinion.

Following *The Cherry Orchard* I went on tour with C K Munro's play, *At Mrs Bean's*, which had enjoyed a long run at that same Royalty Theatre. I was engaged for Jean Cadell's part. I was all for following in her impeccable footsteps but found myself reprimanded for underplaying. The management required a performance in italics and I found the tour pretty hard going. If only they had let me alone I might have given a reasonably good show, but it did teach me something about the difference between trying to reproduce another actress's interpretation and originating one of your own.

Then I had a long spell of understudying. This was in Eden Philpott's *Yellow Sands*, and I understudied Drusilla Wills as one of the egregious twins—a delicious part I never got the chance of playing until I went on tour a year or two later. More reprimands: this time from Ben Greet for my laziness in being content to sit night after night in the understudy room instead of doing constructive work in repertory or on tour. I suppose he was right, but the long months at my favourite theatre, the Haymarket, were very happy in their quiet way. I was among friends, even relations, as H.O. was playing the lawyer—the first and last time we were in a theatre together—and my Bensonian chum, Susan Richmond, was Jennifer, the octogenarian. And it was in *Yellow*

77

Sands that I first met Ralph Richardson. He was quite unknown at that time and seemed to give no promise of the distinguished eccentric actor he was to become. But his lovable personality was always evident, and infuses itself into every character he plays. None of us will forget that wonderful concerted piece of acting he shared with John Gielgud in David Storey's play *Home*, where he and John played two gently deranged characters.

Frank Vosper who played the young Socialist Joe Varwell, was brilliant, dynamic, friendly and occasionally disconcerting. I remember his saying to me 'Why haven't you got on better?' which was probably meant as a somewhat back-handed compliment.

Another of my buddies in *Yellow Sands* was Clarence Blakiston (who was understudying H.O. for whom he played many times when H.O. was in hospital for appendicitis). 'Blakie' stood for a sort of father-figure; he gave me advice, disapproved of my lack of religious beliefs (he was a devout Catholic) and kept me supplied with my two adored luxuries: violets and china tea. At that time I took his affection and indeed every one's for granted, I was arrogant enough to consider it my due. In my old age I've come to realise how precious it is, and am happy and a little surprised when I find it.

During the run of *Yellow Sands* I began my life-long friendship with the Blakelocks who have influenced me in so many ways. Alban and his future wife, Renée, were my close companions in the understudy room and introduced me to Denys and their vicarage home. Subsequently he came to have a special place in my life, for it was he who suggested that I should write these reminiscences. At that time he had just completed his own book, *Round the Next Corner*, so I considered him something of an authority.

Between jobs I used to spend a good deal of time with my two married sisters, Angela and Constance. Constance was by then the mother of six adorable children, and Angela, with her husband, Bernard Green, and their daughter, Antonia, lived in Leamington. She and I used to collaborate in playwriting. She was a leading light at the Loft, an amateur theatre that is still flourishing. If she had been allowed to be an actress—taboo in her youth—I'm sure she would have acted me off the stage. Only one of our plays was performed professionally, this was *Tomorrow's Another Day*, which was put on for a Sunday night performance at the St Martin's Theatre with a really super cast that included Reggie Purdell, Margaretta Scott, Denys Blakelock and Anthony Ireland. We had high hopes, but after a good deal of coming and going they faded out. The play would be too dated now for any chance of being revived. The rest of our efforts were done at the Loft with Angela directing.

In the summer of 1929, I had the offer to go to New York in *Rope*, which was enjoying a successful run in London. Ernest Milton, the only member of the London cast to go to the States, is one of the wittiest, most brilliant actors I have ever met. Renowned for his Hamlet at the Old Vic, his wonderful portrayal of Pirandello's Mock Emperor, and a score of other leading parts, his career in the theatre is a memorable one. During the run of *Rope* he and I became great friends. I've rarely known a more stimulating companion and his wife, Naomi Royde-Smith, herself a celebrated novelist, was in her own way, as witty as Ernest. During our visit to New York she used to take me with her to picture galleries and I learnt a lot from her, both about the art of painting and the art of living.

Rope was an instant success in New York and only the Wall Street disaster prevented our having a long run and a tour to follow. We were all bitterly disappointed for we all had interesting parts. Mine was a lady who might have been completely deaf or completely imbecile, nobody could be sure which. The young Sebastian Shaw played Branden, instigator of the macabre murder.

I must say that I've rarely seen more intoxication than I did in New York in those days, in spite of, or perhaps in consequence of the prohibition laws in force at the time. Ernest took me to a 'Speakeasy'—a daring adventure. All drink was suspect and on one occasion I proved it. While in Boston we were taken to a night-club, an over-heated place where we danced and were plied with the dubious liquor known as Rye Whiskey. Hot and excited and talking away, I failed to notice how often my glass was replenished. By the time we straggled out into the icy air of the small hours we were all terribly unsteady on our feet. Somehow we got back to our hotel and I will draw a veil over the ensuing few minutes. At any rate I registered a vow that if this was being 'tight' then I'd foreswear liquor for the rest of my life. Perhaps my Irish blood derived from a hard-drinking ancestry saved me from any evil results. Next morning I woke with no ill effects beyond a streaming cold. Needless to say that was my one and only experience of a 'gaudy night', but of course I didn't keep strictly to my vow of total abstinence.

In the autumn of 1930 I made my first incursion into musical comedy. It was an amusing trifle called *Blue Roses*, with music by Vivian Ellis and lyrics by Desmond Carter, brother of Nell and Di, two of my greatest friends in the theatre. I had a small speaking part, 'feed' to the comedian, George Clarke. I was a bit scared at first, but George turned out to be a delightfully easy person and it was fun never to be sure what tricks he might be up to. We broke records on tour, but George, an enormous favourite in the provinces, somehow didn't go down with London audiences and our run at the Gaiety Theatre lasted a bare six weeks. I was greatly impressed by the work put in by the cast. Straight acting pales beside the hard labour involved in rehearsing a musical. There were new shibboleths to be learnt. The principals were addressed as 'ladies and gentlemen', the chorus were 'boys and girls'.

I seemed to be dogged by *Yellow Sands*. I had already done a long tour, and then in 1931, Barry Jackson sent out a repertoire of plays to Canada. Once more I was requisitioned for a twin. Most of the other plays were already cast and there remained only the twin and a small part in *Quality Street*, together with some under-studying which I resented but had to put up with if I wanted to go on the tour. It began inauspiciously for me. Part of the publicity was a brochure containing photographs of the company. On opening mine I was confronted with a charming young woman bearing my name but with no other connection with myself. Of course I complained bitterly, but as thousands of these brochures had been printed for distribution, nothing could be done about it so I was obliged to travel from coast to coast under my own name and with someone else's face. In protest, when asked for my autograph I used to scribble my name right across the false face, feeling that thereby I could establish my identity.

The actual touring was thrilling. We played in all the big towns and a good many small ones. Some of the places recalled memories of that other Canadian tour which I was ready to forget. We were a great success and given endless hospitality. Autumn plunged into an achingly cold winter. We endured near-frost-bite, temporary blindness from the carpets of blue snow reflected from cloudless skies, and occasionally fought our way through blizzards. I was longing to turn back and go home, but all the same we were a jolly company and I made a good many friends. An outstanding member of the company was Donald Wolfit, whose creation of the young Robert Browning in *The Barretts of Wimpole Street*, one of the plays in the repertoire, I shall always remember. Some years later, in the musical, *Robert and Elizabeth*, he repeated his success, but this time as the formidable Mr Barrett.

We finished the first half of our Canadian tour with an enchanting three-day train journey through the Rockies, and awoke one morning to find ourselves in Vancouver with rain coming down to remind us of England. A beautiful city, Vancouver, hemmed in by mountains, with Stanley Park adding to its grace. We played there for two weeks and before starting on our return journey, put in a week or two in Victoria which struck me as disappointing: English and old-fashioned English at that. On our way home we took in most of the places we had been to on our way out. It was mid-May when we reached London, green and welcoming, and home.

A week or two after my return, my mother died. She had been ill for some time and her memory had begun to fail, but she retained the indestructible beauty and spirit that made her such a lovable person. So my life took on a different pattern. Elaine, who had looked after my mother ever since my father's death, came to share my London flat. Her vivid personality, her sympathy and quick wit endeared her to everyone.

My next West End venture was with Ernest Milton again, in *Night's Candles*, a translation of Alfred de Musset's *Lorenzaccio*, adapted by May Agate and her husband, Wilfred Grantham. Ernest gave one of his most spectacular performances. I shall always remember him in a black tunic with huge, puffed white sleeves, dominating, romantic and gloriously sinister. My own part, that of a duenna, was nothing remarkable, but it was exciting to be in so distinguished a production. We tried the play out at Fulham in what was then known as the Shilling Theatre. I don't know what metamorphosis it has undergone, but it no longer exists as a theatre. With a few changes of cast we opened at the Queen's Theatre, London. The play ran for only a few weeks: it deserved a better fate. Ann Casson, then in her teens, was in the cast. How well I remember her at the end of a dress rehearsal when we were most of us feeling more than our age; Ann, as tired as anyone, looking very small and about ten.

At that time it was the custom for the cast to take calls after each act, but I think it was discontinued very soon after. An unnecessary and, I think, a disillusioning habit.

Ernest released me from *Lorenzaccio* so that I could appear in *Sunshine Sisters*, whose only claim to fame being that it was, I believe, Ivor Novello's one and only 'flop'. It was a frothy concoction in which I was practically the sole member of the cast who wasn't a musical star. The play contained a good deal of singing and dancing; I, in the role of a clergyman's chatty wife, was of course just a spectator, together with my demure husband. I felt a bit lost in that *galère*, but it gave me the opportunity of meeting Ivor Novello, and like everyone else, I came under the spell of one of the best-loved people in the theatre.

Although we always remained good friends, I'd not acted with Sybil Thorndike since the Old Vic days until 1936 when I went on a long tour with a company composed chiefly of the Casson family: Sybil, Lewis, Christopher and Ann. We did a repertoire of three or four plays, directed by Lewis. By this time I'd ceased to be scared of him, strict disciplinarian though he was. In one play, D H Lawrence's *My Son's my Son*, in which Sybil and I were a couple of Lancashire housewives, I remember Lewis sitting beside me at the rehearsal of a scene demanding some pathos, and saying, 'Don't be sorry for yourself.' I've always tried to profit by that splendid piece of advice. He himself gave a fine performance as the Messenger in *The Hippolytus*. The rest of us doubled and redoubled and the youthful Ann showed great promise as Phaedra. One joyous production was Noël Coward's *Fumed Oak*, where I was the one non-member of the Casson family. The only time I've ever known Lewis to laugh on the stage—unofficially, I mean—was during a performance of this play.

We were in Blackpool, playing *My Son's my Son* on the night of the Abdication. Sybil and I went up to the Circle after the show, still in our shawls and curl-papers, to listen to Edward VIII's farewell broadcast. We were all in tears and I felt that another era of life was past. During the following thirty-six years, we knew little of the Duke and Duchess of Windsor, living their lives away from England, mostly in France. He returned to England on rare occasions: for his mother's funeral; from time to time on a visit to a London Nursing Home for an eye-operation and other less important ailments, but London wasn't his home any more. And now the Epilogue has been written. He died on the twenty-eighth of May, 1972, a few weeks before his seventy-eighth birthday, and in spite of the loss felt by all of us who had idolised him as the Prince of Wales, we could feel he'd come back to his own people. Beneath a picture of the Lying in State in a national newspaper, the caption ran: 'Edward the Eighth comes home from Exile'.

VII

MARKING TIME

My next venture abroad was to go to Paris for a short season, in an adaptation of Radclyffe Hall's novel, *The Well of Loneliness*. In 1930 the book was considered the apotheosis of daring, dealing as it did with a love-affair between two girls. Compared with, let us say, *The Killing of Sister George*, it was completely innocuous. I found the book sentimental and boring but it caused a minor sensation at the time and to procure a copy was a major achievement. The play, I thought, was even below the level of the novel. An American actress, Willette Kershaw, played the part of the heroine, Stephen. She was one of those super-emotional actresses who shed such copious tears on the stage that they swamped her performance. I played her governess and wasn't at all happy. When, after seven weeks at the Potinière Theatre, the season finished, I was intensely relieved. Or course, Paris itself was enchanting. My happiest hours were spent in exploring its beauties, getting re-acquainted with the language and acquiring an accent derived chiefly from waiters and bus conductors. A tentative idea of bringing the play to London was severely censored and it died quietly in Paris after a second season the following year when I was not of the company.

I think it was around this period that I had an unhappy time understudying at the Haymarket in G B Stern's play, *Five Farthings*. I mention this only because it was my one encounter with Dame Marie Tempest. I was terribly badly off and conscious of shabby attire and Marie Tempest's invariably smart appearance did nothing to help. Let me not be too censorious, but she is really the only star I have found 'difficult'. I suppose I was scared of her and she probably sensed this. I admired her perfect technique and dominating presence, but her acting never seemed to have any real heart in it. All the same, she was greatly loved by those who really knew her, so maybe I'm just prejudiced.

It was in this year that John Gielgud was giving his unsurpassed performance in *Hamlet* at the Queen's Theatre. Simultaneously the German actor, Moissi, was at the Globe, also playing the part. The two performances couldn't really bear comparison. Moissi's conception was lacking in depth, so it seemed to me; I'm sure he was better suited to comedy, though I do recall the touching cadence of his '*Mutti!*' in the Closet scene and his striking appearance. Also in that production was the most beautiful Ophelia I have ever seen. Alec Guinness's Hamlet, in Tyrone Guthrie's modern dress production at the Vic, was very young and touching. The scene starting with 'How all occasions' (so often cut) I remember particularly. I didn't see his second Hamlet at the Old Vic in 1937. John Byron, who played at Stratford-upon-Avon, gave a most lovable performance. His 'Rest, rest, perturbed spirit' is another beautiful line to remember. An interesting experiment was Barry Jackson's modern dress production, the first, I think, of the modern dress classics to reach London. Colin Keith-Johnstone's Hamlet I didn't find particularly convincing; he never suggested royalty—perhaps the modern garb of the 1930s accounted for that.

While I was in New York I saw Jean-Louis Barrault as Hamlet, beautiful and full of pathos, but a little too exotic to suggest the underlying strength of the character. My father used to say Hamlet was a madman pretending to be mad but I think he was utterly wrong. If you read the play with the slightest insight, you must surely realise there is no doubt of Hamlet's sanity throughout. He gives innumerable proofs of it. Close on his first encounter with his father's ghost, he gives his friends this warning:

> 'How strange or odd soe'er I bear myself
> As I perchance hereafter shall think meet
> To put an antic disposition on . . .'

Later, his conversation with Rosencranz and Guilden-
stern betrays no sign of madness; his two soliloquies: 'O,
what a rogue' and 'To be or not to be . . .' are the
reflections of a man completely in command of himself;
just before the Play Scene, he talks to Horatio with the
deep understanding of a man of reason. Off and on
during the whole action of the play, he indulges in his
predicted 'antic disposition', with long interludes reveal-
ing his true self, concluding with his short scene with
Horatio before the fatal duel. I don't know why there
should be any doubt of Hamlet's essential sanity. I have
only faint, schoolgirl memories of Matheson Lang and
Martin Harvey in the part and was too young to
criticise Benson. Having seen so many interpretations I
find comparing them fascinating and I do maintain that
no *Hamlet* can be so bad that there isn't something good
for you to carry away.

To pursue the subject of acting throughout the ages:
the other day, going through some old papers, I came
upon a cutting from the *Era*, a theatrical publication
long since defunct, but in my time a sort of younger
sister of *The Stage*. It was an article written by my
brother, H.O. and the year was 1927. Comparing the
style of acting in his day with that of thirty years before,
when he first appeared on the stage in the Benson
Company, he says:

'In the Company, unless an artist proved himself a
fairly competent performer, he was of no use to us
then. But we didn't discuss our art. We never talked
shop, we never spoke about our Press notices—when
one did he was snubbed and this had a salutary effect
because he wasn't allowed to get a swollen head and
that made for good acting. In the Benson Company
we most of us played games and I think the sporting

atmosphere had a great deal to do with the way we all pulled together. This same atmosphere unfortunately doesn't obtain any more, because in these days of syndicates there are so few actor-managers. It would be a blessing if they could return, for in the actor-manager you always had somebody to take a personal interest in you. Another thing: the pace of acting has become more rapid. In the early days actors were inclined to 'Pong' out their words, but I think they overdo things nowadays by trying to be too natural. In these days actors speak Shakespeare rather like machine-guns and miss the poetry to a great extent. Really I think Shakespearean acting today is largely inferior to that of say twenty years ago. In modern work I think it a pity that so many inexperienced youngsters are placed in big parts before they are ready for them. Twenty years ago that wasn't the case. Actors were expected to have some experience of touring. They had to learn gradually. Sir Henry Irving sent one of his sons on tour with Benson before allowing him to join his own company.' Speaking of modern plays, he continues: 'In the last twenty years the type of play has altered considerably. Today one sees so many dealing with sex problems. They have taken the place of old comedies which, if not first class drama, were at least clean and wholesome. The change has come about since the war,'— He is of course referring to the First World War— 'and I am not sure that the cinema has not altered the dramatic taste of the public. I think drama is in danger of being killed by the pictures. Since the war I have felt that theatregoers have become rather amoral. It doesn't matter what they see, they just don't care. But my opinion is that "sex" plays will die out in time.'

Thus an actor, who were he alive today would be close on a hundred: to the present generation his 'today' is history. This article may sound a trifle archaic and sententious, yet on reading it over I seem to find one or two points not irrelevant to our own time. But will 'sex' plays die out? I think not. There have always been sex plays. What about *Othello*? However, some day the present obsession with nudity may start feeling the chill, and wrap up, in more senses than one.

Television, now a familiar feature of every household, made its difficult birth around the end of 1936. Its headquarters were the Alexandra Palace, known to us as the Ally Pally. My first performance was in February, 1937, in Noël Coward's *Hands Across the Sea*, and a strange experience it was. We used to give two shows, live of course, with an interval of two or three days—time enough to go through a second attack of first-night nerves. Make-up, now almost negligible, was odd and lurid—a sort of bright yellow. Performances were all very intimate and congested. You and your fellow-actors huddled together to get into the picture, with someone almost at your feet holding the prompt book, though a prompt was considered a shocking affair. Later on a 'stop-key' was invented. This contraption shut off sound for the split second in which the artist could repeat the necessary word or line. Viewers might be conscious of a slight hiatus and put it down to a fault in the set: thus the wretched actor's reputation would be saved.

A tour of the *Six Men of Dorset* followed hard upon this: a very moving play about the Tolpuddle martyrs. I played the youthful daughter of Sybil and Lewis, incredible as this must sound. I don't suppose anyone but Lewis would have thought me capable of such an anachronism, and I felt acutely embarrassed when at rehearsal the stage-manager remarked, 'You're not going to *play* the part, are you?' But I had such faith in Lewis that I was ready to have a go at anything he might suggest. As a matter of fact, with the aid of judicious make-up and dress, I was able to get away with it, and quite surprised members of the audience when they realised who the young person really was.

The tour, sponsored by the TUC, involved us in a plethora of political meetings. One of the principal speakers was the late James Maxton, beloved of his colleagues whatever their politics. We were entertained at tea parties, were taken over all manner of factories, and caught the infection of Socialism from the Cassons who were in their element and often spoke at the meetings. We belonged to the Left Book Club and the *Daily Worker* was our daily bread. Since then my politics have modified, though I still have a bias towards the Left.

All this time war clouds were gathering. The name of Adolf Hitler loomed large in the news. Antonia Green, Angela's daughter, came home from studying singing in Dresden, loud in her praise of this wonderful man who was going to restore the fortunes of Germany. 'Hitler Youth' was to play an important part in the country's resurrection. Hitler himself was depicted as a holy man whose constant companion was the Bible. Much as I love Antonia I simply couldn't join in these eulogies, so soon to be dispelled.

During this ominous period I went back to the Vic for a couple of productions. It was jolly to be there again after twenty years. By that time Lilian Baylis had died and Tyrone Guthrie was directing. His exciting method and the years of experience behind me gave me a good deal more confidence than I'd known under the banner of Ben Greet, to say nothing of Miss Baylis, with whom I was never wholly at ease. It was rather comforting to be no longer aware of her vigilant presence in the stage-box.

We were playing *Trelawny of the Wells* at the time of the Munich crisis, when Chamberlain lulled the nation into the spurious 'Peace in our time'. O B Clarence and I were Aunt Trafalgar and her brother Sir William, Sophie Stewart was Rose and Alec Guinness Arthur Gower. I shall never forget the night of Neville Chamberlain's broadcast on the eve of his first visit to Hitler. We gathered on the stage to listen, just before the show. I can still see Anthony Quayle standing there, spreading greasepaint on his anxious face.

Remnants of the crisis stayed with us. Sandbags in the streets, ominous newspaper articles and a general atmosphere of feverish hopes and fears. In the summer of 1939 I was at the Swansea Repertory Theatre in a new play. I spent my free time on those glorious summer days, swimming or going for walks in the lovely Welsh country, surrounded by peaceful scenes but dogged always by a sense of impending disaster. Children were being evacuated to the country. On our opening night I was presented with a small cardboard box. 'Flowers', thought I. 'How nice.' The box contained my gas-mask.

The play finished abruptly on the second of September, and on the third, during my journey home, war was declared. As I stepped out of the train at Paddington, a porter greeted me with, "'E's been over!' and I sped home, rather expecting to find family and home in pieces. Of course it was just one of the many false alarms we were treated to in those early days. That same evening there was another alert. For some reason we took it to be a gas attack and out came our gas-masks, those grotesque creations that were to become part of our daily equipment. At first a visit to the cinema always included this companion, often borrowed in haste from some obliging friend. In church it sat on your knee, you took walks with it clinging to your shoulder, but as time went on, the gas-mask became a toy that nobody bothered to play with, and all through the years that followed, it was never, thank God, put to serious use.

The long, golden summer wore itself away. There were some tragic disasters at sea, but at home nothing happened to disturb the 'phoney war' and we were lulled into the false belief that nothing ever would happen. Elaine and I spent a month or two at Lady Benson's house in Kensington, to keep it warm while she was in the country, staying with Dick. As a change from our tiny flat we rather enjoyed ourselves. In my free time, which was abundant just then, I did a good deal of story-writing and joined a class at the City Literary Institute. Then, just before Christmas, I went up to Blackpool for the try-out of a new play about journalism, *Behind the Schemes*, sponsored by my old friend Hubert Woodward. Ronald Shiner, then almost unknown, was in it and Franklyn Dyall the star. Blackpool has an odd charm that exerts itself only in winter. It is good to walk along the immense stretch of sand and to wander round the almost noiseless streets. It becomes unendurable only when spring brings in the Season with its welter of picture-postcards, icecream vendors, fortune tellers and day trippers.

Back in London we enjoyed our last 'peaceful' Christmas. Then, just as the New Year was about to be born, Sir Frank Benson died. He was eighty-one and had retired from public life some time before. His Memorial Service at St Martin-in-the-Fields is something to remember. So many Old Bensonians (some of them really old) were there. H.O. was one of the ushers. I think it was Henry Ainley who read the Lessons and Frank Cochrane sang. These are with us no longer. Not a great collection of us left. Although I hadn't seen Sir Frank for many years, I was always conscious of his influence on my career as a beginner, and his death seemed a goodbye to an important part of my life.

By that time Lady Benson was back in London, and Elaine and I returned to Great Newport Street, where we performed the incredibly boring task of re-hanging the black-out curtains, making the best of the long winter, glad of the spurious monotony and yet all the time restless with foreboding of what might be in store.

And then it was 1940 and Neville Chamberlain blithely announced that Hitler had 'missed the bus'. But all too soon he caught the next one and the war flared up into spectacular being.

VIII

OXFORD IN WARTIME

The Battle of Britain was in full spate. Elaine and I had just moved into a new flat; a pleasant small haven in Royal Hospital Road, not far from the Chelsea Hospital. We'd often come across an old Pensioner, grizzled and red-coated, and sometimes on a Sunday would go to the fascinating church, and more often would picnic in the surrounding garden. Barrage balloons rocked in the perpetually blue sky, their impersonal calm undisturbed even by the dogfights between planes that were becoming increasingly frequent and alarming.

For the moment I was turning down offers of work as I was immersed in typing a book—*King's Masque*, by Evan John, a magnificent piece of work about the French Revolution. I had scarcely finished this and was beginning to think about the stage again, when H.O. was taken suddenly ill. I think it was natural that the war immediately took second place. Our anxiety was concentrated on our brother, and when I had an offer from the Oxford Playhouse to act for a few weeks in a couple of productions, I was extremely reluctant to leave London, and accepted the offer with some misgivings. I'd been there earlier in the year for two plays directed by Leslie French, an old friend of mine, and years ago I'd done a matinée of *The Cherry Orchard* at the little old Repertory Theatre in the Woodstock Road. This had lately been superceded by the new Playhouse in Beaumont Street, a charming theatre, run by Eric Dance until he was called up. I was disappointed to hear that Leslie had been succeeded by a new director, Christopher Fry, a name unknown to me. I arrived at the theatre to rehearse my old part in *Rope*, not inclined to approve of my new director. I don't have to say that within a week prejudice died and a friendship was born, which

flourishes to this day. The two weeks extended themselves. Rather like that legendary curate who went out
to tea, consumed with shyness and found himself unable
to leave ¡until compelled by his own funeral, I came
to Oxford for a fortnight and stayed five years. Those
years marked a new departure in my way of life.

Occasionally I would go to London for the day and
nearly always arrived together with an air-raid warning.
One sad occasion was H.O.'s funeral. He died a week or
two after I'd established myself at the Playhouse. He
had never really recovered from an acute attack of
pneumonia a few years earlier, and though he had
continued to work, chiefly at the BBC, his health had
suffered. In those days of his earlier illness, Elaine and I
lived in a wretched mixture of hope and fear. At last I
found myself quoting David's cry: 'Is it well with the
Child? It is well,' and that meant that the child was
dead. My grief was so full of self that I felt I could bear
to lose him rather than go on in this state of despair. He
was old enough to be my father and had filled the blank
left by my own father's death so many years ago. He had
stood by me during the most tragic crisis of my life,
with an understanding that perhaps my father wouldn't
have been able to give. He settled the bills that my
incurable extravagance were for ever incurring, bought
me clothes, paid for my holidays and never reproached
me. When he died, my grief, though deep, was less
poignant than in those days of his first illness. He was
safely gathered in; the war couldn't hurt him any more.
Bad weather wouldn't matter—he'd not be catching a
chill. If he was my father, perhaps in a way I was his
mother.

My first year at Oxford brought more losses. My
eldest brother died the following summer, Constance in
October after what had become a tragic life. She lost
her husband and eventually five of her six children
leaving only Veronica, whom I came to love as my own
daughter. She inherited her mother's gallant outlook on

life and became a great source of strength and advice to me.

It seemed my fate to attend a funeral and come back to Oxford to play in a farce. Perhaps the effort helped to keep me going. I came home for a week-end to help Elaine pack H.O.'s belongings, a mournful job strangely enlivened by an air-raid warning. Down we went to the makeshift shelter in the basement where our peace was disturbed more by the intermittent snores of our fellow-victims than by the noise of the raid itself. We laughed *sotto voce* to ourselves. Our flat suffered a good deal of damage in 1941 when so much of Chelsea was hit by a landmine. We weren't in London at the time—fortunately for us, as the flat was littered with broken glass and most of the doors were blown off their hinges.

At Oxford I lived in super digs kept by Mrs Ling in Walton Street. 'Ting-a-Ling', as she was known to us all, was as important a figure as any in the Company. She was everybody's friend, especially mine. Her sitting-room is still spoken of as 'Nixon's room'. All through the war she managed to feed us splendidly, and was ever-lastingly good-tempered. Since the war she has catered almost exclusively for under-graduates, one of them being no less than the son of Harold Wilson, then Prime Minister. The boy said nothing about his august parentage and no one was more surprised than Mrs Ling when she received a call from them and their identity was disclosed. I think she took a fancy to Mrs Wilson but wasn't greatly impressed by the Prime Minister.

My first three months, until Christopher Fry was called up, were spent in hard work and play. I don't know which I enjoyed more. No time for story-writing. The day was devoted to rehearsing, the night to study, for it was weekly rep. I'd spend long afternoons lying under a tree in Worcester garden, a dispatch-case for my pillow, alternately learning lines and dozing. I would go home after the show on a Friday night, still with two performances in front of me, realise I didn't know a line of next week's Act Three and tell myself, 'Oh well, it's only Friday.' With getting on for thirty years between then and now, I marvel at such complacence.

We dress-rehearsed on Sunday nights, often well into the small hours, and Tuesday morning found us reading through next week's play, with last night's first performance, doubtless imperfectly learnt, pushed into the background. Our stage-manager was Diana Harris. She couldn't have been more than about eighteen but she displayed an authority far beyond her years. At first I was inclined to resent her 'Sergeant-major' conduct, but later on we became the dearest of friends and to this day she addresses me as 'Mum'. Many are the times when from her seat in the prompt-corner she has saved me from a disastrous 'dry'. I'd never done weekly rep. before, and starting it when I was no longer young it had a splendid effect on my memory. Whatever the standard of my performances may be, I haven't much difficulty in learning lines, thanks to those years at Oxford.

We did every kind of play from Aldwych farce to Ibsen. Pamela Brown, then about twenty, gave her tremendous performance in *Hedda Gabler*. I've seen several Heddas since, but nobody has spoken the line, 'I'm burning your child' with such effect. James Agate gave her a magnificent notice in the *Sunday Times*. He was staying in Oxford for a few weeks and sometimes came to supper with John Byron and me. I found him an endearing personality; there was nothing pompous about him. He even allowed us the privilege of watching him doze off after an evening of supper and talk. I was anxious to play the wife in *John Gabriel Borkman* and asked what he thought of the idea. 'Well,' he said, regarding me critically, 'You might give a curdled version of the milk of human kindness.' My ambition fortunately died after that.

I shared a dressing-room with Winifred Evans, who

was a wonderful solace. Whatever the state of her own nerves she exercised a soothing influence on mine. On a first night just before I went on the stage, heart a-flutter and hands trembling, she would murmur, *'Dominus Vobiscum'* and I'd invariably calm down.

When I first arrived, Anthony Holland was our scenic designer. He was succeeded by Tanya Moiseiwitsch, daughter of the pianist, and later on her place was taken by the youthful J. Hutchinson Scott. All these three are now famous in the theatre. It's heartening to think of the many reputations made at Oxford.

Our audiences, composed mostly of undergraduates and evacuees, loved us all and were indulgent with our many discrepancies. I dried stone dead on the first night of *The Corn is Green*, in which I was having a shot at Sybil's part. Deafened with nerves, I failed to hear the prompt, called out a despairing 'What?' and then sailed through without further ado. Constant in the audience was John McBennett, a young and reluctant member of the Forces and stationed near Oxford. Our first meeting, when he called at my digs at supper-time and I magnanimously sacrificed my one and only rationed egg, set a seal on a friendship which has continued through the years.

Another friend I made while at Oxford was Caryl Brahms, later celebrated as wit, dramatic critic and already the author of many enchanting novels, notably *Don't, Mr. Disraeli*, a delicious extravaganza which she wrote with the late S J Simon. But it is her fantasy, *Titania has a Mother*, which in my opinion ranks above Grimm and even Hans Andersen.

Perhaps I arrogate to myself a deeper understanding of Caryl than I should. It may be because, in spite of the considerable stretch of years that lies between us, we are in a sense twins. Our birthdays fall on consecutive days: we are Sagittarians. According to the astrologists, Sagittarians are addicts of outdoor sports and animals— one of their mistakes, I think. But they are sadly true in stating that we are obliged to work hard to make a living. Caryl bears this out *in excelsis*. I've never known a more devoted adherent to the grindstone. Her secretary, too, puts in a full-time job, as Caryl cannot spell and cannot add.

In the Oxford days she was young and hadn't quite found herself. She felt it essential to make an impression. Fortified by a cigarette in an elongated holder, she would express herself in rather over-confident terms that seemed to conceal an innate insecurity. But today all these italics have disappeared. She has arrived, though she would tell you she is still travelling hopefully. Her journey lies up and down thorny paths. One day she is affluent and a reckless spender, the next she is terrified to look at her bank balance. Her generosity is boundless, not only in the matter of possessions, it extends to her deep understanding of her fellow men and women. Our friendship has ripened and never wavered.

One memorable performance was Christopher's production of *Pride and Prejudice*, in which I, a somewhat miscast Mrs Bennett, was the proud mother of Pamela Brown, Yvonne Mitchell and Joan Greenwood, all potential stars. George Hannam-Clark played Mr Bennett, and John Byron was Darcy.

Sometimes on a free evening Christopher would read me bits of his new play, *The Firstborn*, a beautiful piece of work that has had many public performances. *The Lady's Not for Burning* hadn't even reached her cradle, and Christopher himself was comparatively unknown. He and his wife, Phyl, had a cottage near Oxford where I spent an occasional week-end and made the acquaintance of their very small son, Tam, now married, a father, and firmly established at the BBC.

Christopher, John Byron and I used to frequent Blackwell's bookshop, browse there for hours on end and usually wind up by giving each other books. It was a commonplace for us to say to each other, 'You haven't given me a book for ages.' On one occasion I hit on a second-hand book about Henry II which was instrumental in leading Christopher to write his play, *Curtmantle*, so I feel a proprietary interest in it. It was produced at the Aldwych Theatre in 1962, a very fine play but I thought it suffered through miscasting and I greatly preferred reading it. Sometimes I think Christopher's plays are like *The Tempest*, more honoured in the reading than in the performance. They do need such perfect casting.

My favourite part of all time was Juno in O'Casey's *Juno and the Paycock*. My father's Irish came in handy, as it has in many other Irish plays. Malcolm Morley, a lovable teddy bear of a man, directed it. He and Peter Ashmore usually directed on alternate weeks.

A chapter about the Playhouse wouldn't be complete without at least a page devoted to Peter Ashmore, our director-in-chief from 1941 until nearly the end of the war. At his best he was brilliant—I don't believe he had a worst, at Oxford, at any rate. He joined us originally as an actor and gave some memorable performances. His Shylock in his own modern-dress *Merchant* was one of the finest I've seen and I've sat through a good few. He looked like a twentieth-century company promoter, was delightfully funny and deeply moving. Another outstanding performer was John Woodnutt, a lanky youth of seventeen who worked his way up from assistant stage-manager to playing important parts. His Lancelot Gobbo was a triumph for a beginner. Speaking of time to come, I once asked him that if I ever became celebrated enough to deserve a Memorial Service, would he be an usher? To which he eagerly responded, 'Rather! I shall look forward to that!' Friendly, if a little surprising.

As a director Peter Ashmore was dynamic. Essentially temperamental, yet he knew what he was after and had a genius for extracting a subtle something from his actors that they were not aware of possessing. He would arrive at rehearsal, inexcusably late, stroll about the stalls with one eye firmly fixed on the stage, the other more often than not, concealed behind an eyebath. He would call us 'Dearheart' but beneath that velvety exterior an iron will was in action. His criticisms were ruthless. Many of my own performances came under his sardonic censure, but if he did approve of anything I did, I could be sure the praise was more or less deserved. We had nicknames for each other: mine for him was 'Speciousness', his for me, 'Mordancy'. If ever I hear mutual friends saying 'Isn't Nora sweet?', I refer them to Peter Ashmore.

Frank Shelley, whom I had known when playing in *Six Men of Dorset*, directed after Peter had left for the wider but less kindly field of the West End. We had a variety of visiting directors, none of them approaching Peter for sheer talent. As for the Company, there was a nucleus of old residents and a multitude of visiting artists; it would take a whole chapter to enumerate them all.

Michael Flanders, a promising young undergraduate, joined as an amateur for one or two productions. He was all set to become a professional when the war was over. He left us to join the Navy, survived a tragic illness and finally became one of our most celebrated entertainers: a marvellous example of talent and courage overcoming what seemed to be disaster.

I quote from a letter he sent me while I was still at Oxford and he in hospital:

'. . . My apologies for the typewriter which I have to use till they get my left thumb working. (Of course my hands are unaffected except for the left thumb, and I would have to be left-handed!) . . . I'm up in the old wheel-chair again, now, pushing round doing a *Man who Came to Dinner* act in my six-months' old beard. This latter is not so silky as Peter's (has he it still?) but it is black and red, which is rather distinguished... There was a semi-political society when I was up that used to operate from Magdalen. Sidney Keyes, the Hawthornden prizewinner, killed in Libya, belonged. They used to call themselves the National Liberals or some such name, but all they did each term was to call a casting meeting for *Winterset*. I attended every one because I would have given my soul to play "Mio!". Anyway they always told me I would make a better "Shadow". It never came off, but I used to look in the mirror and think, "Do I really only look like a 'Mio' to me, and a shadow to everyone else?" Write and tell me I'm wrong, there's a dear. I shan't be able to play it now, anyway. Yes, I'm afraid Gielgud and Olivier are safe as far as I'm concerned. But as long as you remember I was the man who said, "No Caroline, Miss Brandy?" that's something...'

The war continued to rage, while we in Oxford lived in comparative peace. At the Playhouse our only contribution to hostilities was the nightly fire-watching. Four of us took a weekly turn, spending uncomfortable hours on improvised beds in the dressing-rooms, and on hot summer nights dragging our mattresses on to the flat roof. No activities were demanded of us, a piece of good fortune, though we imagined we'd have welcomed an occasional air-raid. So life in the theatre pursued its customary daily and nightly round. When I happened to be out of a play I used to spend week-ends at Chipping Campden where Elaine and Angela were living at that time. Campden, unlike its commercialised neighbour, Broadway, was completely unspoilt; an ideal place for a holiday. We were given one week's holiday with pay; a second week was allowed, at our own expense. The Playhouse salaries were minute: an occasional bonus helped, and Mrs Ling's weekly bills were generously small.

Every year we used hopefully to say, 'Next year the war will be over' and of course year after year went by, sometimes bringing us to wild optimism, sometimes to near despair. And then at last it really was over. The eighth of May, 1945. Unbelievably true. Universal rejoicing and a holiday for everyone it seemed—save for us at the Playhouse. We rehearsed just as usual.

The next excitement was the General Election, with Churchill ousted and Clement Attlee taking his place. Essentially a man of war, the nation wasn't able to regard Churchill as a peacemaker. Although he was re-elected later on, his great days were over. To the present generation he is more or less a legend, much as Lloyd George appears to the middle-aged of today. For myself, my memory of Prime Ministers goes back to the death of Gladstone in 1898, vague though it is. Names like Campbell Bannerman, Balfour and Ramsay Macdonald are as remote as King Canute, and Baldwin is probably remembered chiefly for his concern with the Abdication in 1936. But for all his withdrawal from public life, Churchill's death was his resurrection. From the Queen herself down to the humblest of us sitting in tears round our television sets, the whole nation played a vital part in his State Funeral in St Paul's Cathedral. A great British Statesman, perhaps the last of them.

Then came the fifteenth of August; when we defeated Japan with the splitting of the atom and the devastating bomb on Hiroshima, an event that filled some of us with elation and many of us with shame. Could we call it Peace with Honour?

All through the autumn, life at Oxford went on its usual way. Then just before Christmas I felt it was time I said goodbye to the Playhouse. But it wasn't really goodbye as from time to time I came back for one or two productions. It still held its magic. Now it has undergone vast changes, for the better, most people say. I went up to see a performance of *Juno and the Paycock* not long ago, and felt some of the magic was lacking. Perhaps I had changed as well as the theatre. Eric Dance, who started it all, died as a prisoner-of-war in Japanese hands before he could know what a proud position the

Ronald Shiner and myself in *Behind the Schemes*,
1940.

Lady Sneerwell in *The School for Scandal*, Oxford
Playhouse, with Winifred Evans and David Green.

The Lady's Not for Burning, in America, 1950, with John Gielgud and Pamela Brown.

Alma Taylor in *Comin' Thro' the Rye,* 1923.

Christopher Fry in recent years.

Virginia McKenna
as Jean Paget
with me as Mrs
Frith in *A Town
Like Alice*, 1956.

Claire Bloom as
Nora in *A Doll's
House*, 1973.

Fay Compton as Aunt Ann, Fanny Rowe as Emily, Nora Swinburne as Aunt Hester and me as Aunt Juley in *The Forsyte Saga*, 1967.

Relaxing during rehearsals for *Forty Years On* with Alan Bennett and Sir John Gielgud, 1968.

Playhouse was to hold amongst repertories. In the vestibule there is a plaque erected to his memory.

My last week at the Playhouse is one I shall always remember. I had given my final performance in an aura of presents, speeches and tears, and was actually packing up to leave Oxford almost immediately. On Tuesday night up came a message from the Playhouse. One of the cast had been taken suddenly ill and of course there was no understudy. Would I come down and read the part? It was really alarming. I'd been in front on the Monday night but knew very little about the play. But there was no alternative. Spectacles on nose, book in one hand while the other was hampered with endless props, to say nothing of being further encumbered with a West-country accent, on I went, and somehow got through without mishap. I was prevailed on to finish the week, but on one condition: I refused to learn the lines. Consequently I went on every night grasping the script, amid subdued jeers from the rest of the company.

IX
DISCOVERED AT LAST!

I felt I deserved a holiday after that, and took one, though not for long as in the New Year I went to the Bristol Old Vic, its first repertory season, with Hugh Hunt directing. Two of my Playhouse chums, Pamela Brown and Yvonne Mitchell, were in the Company, and our beloved Tanya Moiseiwitsch. I think the Theatre Royal, Bristol is the most beautiful theatre in England, and added to its beauty it has the ghost of Sarah Siddons and several others to its credit, though I'm thankful to say, I never encountered any of them.

The men of the Bristol Old Vic Company were mostly youngsters, lately demobbed. Perhaps that accounted for the slight atmosphere of unease that pervaded that first season. Everyone seemed the victim of nerves, and Hugh Hunt's job couldn't have been particularly rewarding. William Devlin and Noel Willman played most of the leads and were excellent foils for each other.

During the season we performed *The Beaux Stratagem*, *Macbeth*, with Pamela Brown as Lady Macbeth giving one of her best and most original performances. I played Lady Bountiful in *The Beaux Stratagem* and First Witch in *Macbeth*. Then we did *Jenny Villiers*, a new play by J B Priestley, depicting the adventures of a theatrical stock company in the last century. Not one of Mr Priestley's best, but interesting in its fairy-tale way. I was woefully miscast as the 'heavy', there being nobody else of the right age. J B Priestley who came down to supervise rehearsals, remarked to me, 'Your part should be played by someone like Clara Butt', and how right he was. All the same we got a good deal of fun out of the play, more perhaps than the author intended.

I enjoyed working for Hugh Hunt, whom I've always found sympathetic and understanding. Towards the end of the season we put on a production of *Weep for the Cyclops*, Denis Johnston's play about Dean Swift. I played the faithful Rebecca Dingley and Bill Devlin was very moving as the Mad Dean. Swift has always been one of my heroes. When in Dublin I love to wander round the precincts of St Patrick's Cathedral and picture the great man going about his avocations.

Bristol is the most fascinating city. It was then recovering slowly from its war wounds and there were great gaps among the buildings. Now that it has been largely rebuilt it seems to have lost a little of its character.

In the autumn I was back at Bristol to rehearse Ronald Gow's adaptation of *Tess of the D'Urbervilles* in which his wife, Wendy Hiller, gave a beautiful performance. We did a week at the New Theatre, vacated for the moment by the London Old Vic company, toured for a while and finally came to the Piccadilly Theatre for a short run. There was a young man playing the part of a shepherd whom I marked down for stardom, and sure enough, the young man, Paul Rogers, fulfilled my prediction.

Tess wasn't a specially exciting engagement, but through it I made a valuable friendship with Felix de Wolfe. It was *Tess* that brought me to his notice and for twenty-five years he has been my agent and close friend. Both in and out of the theatre I find him a stimulating influence. It's the fashion for actors to swop experiences of their agents and very often they are not terribly complimentary. I'm fortunate enough to be in the position of boasting that mine is the best agent in London.

Early in 1947 I had heard through Christopher Fry of a first play by Wynyard Browne, *Dark Summer*, about a man blinded in the war and the women in his life. There was a part in it that both he and Christopher wanted me to play, and Frith Banbury, who was to direct it, was of the same opinion. But the management, H M Tennent, wasn't so keen. It wasn't until several actresses had turned it down for various reasons, that it fell finally to me, and what a good part it was, that of an inquisitive and garrulous spinster. We were a small cast, which included Jean Cadell and Joan Miller. Frith directed it beautifully. We did a short tour and then went for a week to Holland, playing most of the capitals.

We had a wonderful week. It surprised us that so soon after the appalling times they had been through, the food was so good and plentiful. Steaks galore, and the splendid cream cakes that had disappeared from England since 1939. At home rationing continued and we were grateful for food parcels that still came from America. From Kenya my nephew, Peter Silver, sent us a ham of such noble proportions that none of our saucepans could hold it. Our newsagent, a friendly neighbour, volunteered to cook it and we gladly consented, on condition that she kept half for herself. Some time later, she told me she had boiled it in the foot-bath used by herself and her nephew, a somewhat unappetising gentleman of middle-age. We were relieved that we'd been spared the knowledge until the ham had had its day.

In spite of its swift recovery, the bomb damage brought home to us how deeply Holland had suffered, and how fortunate we had been in escaping invasion. We played at Rotterdam, its wounds still gaping, and on a visit to Enskerde, where residents put us up for the night, we learnt some of the horrors of war. I stayed with a young couple with whom I still exchange Christmas greetings. At first I didn't like to speak of the war, it seemed like prying into a recent bereavement, but after the show that night they told me of their experiences. A few had their humorous side. For instance, the children, when asked the way by a German, would gleefully send him in the opposite direction. But the stories of those nightly terrors when a knock at the door meant an enemy caller gave us a deeper insight into what these brave people went through.

Some years later on holiday in Amsterdam I visited the tragic Anne Frank's house, stood in the room where the family had lived for so long, and saw the pathetic pictures that Anne had stuck on the walls. There was a postcard of the two little English Princesses. In spite of their gaiety the war seems close to the Dutch people even now.

The Dutch theatres were very comfortable but the Continental habit of having a *Lange Pause* halfway through a performance was a trifle disconcerting. Members of the audience would come backstage for a chat, and after half an hour of this you were inclined to lose the thread of the play.

We returned to London and opened at the Lyric, Hammersmith, for a short season. Hidden away among a welter of market-stalls in a Hammersmith side-street, this pretty little theatre gained huge support in the twenties through Nigel Playfair's production of *The Beggar's Opera*. All London flocked to see it. Now, after many great seasons, it has suffered the fate of several of our theatres—I don't know whether it is actually pulled down or has been put to some industrial misuse. I had already played there, in a somewhat regrettable production of *Macbeth* in which I was one of the witches. At different times I've played all three of them. In spite of backstage drawbacks and the sound of trains rumbling past, I was glad to be at the Lyric once more.

After the first night of *Dark Summer* the management was very nice and encouraging about my performance. I think they considered me a discovery. Oh dear, I'd been in and out of the West End for quite a while, longer perhaps than some of my employers. I cast my mind back to my clairvoyante friend in the Terry company who had predicted success years ago. *Dark Summer* was the beginning of a long association with H M Tennent. 'Binkie' and John Perry thoroughly made up for all their early misgivings about me.

After the Lyric Hammersmith we transferred to the St Martin's and had a run of a few months. Soon after that I was in a play at the New Lindsay, one of London's

Little Theatres that flourished at this period. These theatres, useful as 'shop-windows', are coming into their own again as the birthplace of many a play that has gone on to the West End. This particular play, *Corinth House*, was by Pamela Hansford Johnson, so well known as a novelist. It was the interesting study of an ex-schoolmistress whose life was nearly wrecked by the machinations of one of her pupils who considered herself grievously wronged. I played the schoolmistress, Miss Malleson, an excellent part, though playing it to an audience in close proximity to the stage rather took from my enjoyment. One night, in the throes of a dramatic scene demanding the utmost concentration, my attention was drawn suddenly to a pair of feet resting on the edge of the stage. Looking a few inches further, I traced their owner, lolling comfortably in the front row of the stalls. Quite disturbing, but after all, players in Shakespeare's day had many such distractions to contend with. The New Lindsay is replaced now by a block of flats.

In the spring, just before *Corinth House*, I had made my first film of any importance—*The Blue Lagoon*. Donald Houston, who had been with me at Oxford, and the youthful Jean Simmons, were the stars. I had the small part of Jean's aunt. People say that if during an engagement you hear the cuckoo, you are sure to return to that locality before long. In my case I heard him during *The Blue Lagoon*, and sure enough was back at Pinewood in the autumn in *Fools Rush In*; a harassing assignment as I was currently playing at the Globe in *The Return of the Prodigal*, a revival of an old play by St John Hankin, so well known in his day as a writer for the Gaiety, Manchester. I lived in terror of being late for a performance. *The Prodigal* had only a limited run but we all enjoyed ourselves, chiefly perhaps because the cast was headed by Sybil and John. Irene Browne was also in the cast. She had the reputation of being 'difficult' but I never found her so. I think the presence of Sybil had that cheering effect she has on everyone she acts with. At the

Memorial Service after Irene's death, Emlyn Williams gave the address. I remember him saying that being with Irene was rather like the weather—you were never quite sure what to wear in her company. But it was lovingly said.

As soon as *The Prodigal* finished we embarked on rehearsals for Christopher Fry's *The Lady's Not for Burning*, my favourite of all his plays, except *The Boy with a Cart*, his first and I think his most beautiful. It was largely through Christopher that I was given the part of Margaret Devize, one of the most rewarding I have ever played. She was a person of some consequence, but a personality quite inconsequential. To quote one of her characteristic lines:

> 'One day I shall burst my bud
> Of calm and blossom into hysteria'

And another—a sentiment I fervently endorse:

> 'I could do with a splendid holiday
> In a complete vacuum.'

The Lady had a distinguished cast. John, who also directed, was Thomas Mendip, the soldier with a penchant for death. Jennet Jourdemayne, the so-called witch marked down for burning, but in love with life, was Pamela Brown. Christopher had written the part for her and she brought to it her own special beauty and grace. It was the third time she and I had been together in the theatre. Harcourt Williams, hero of my youth, was my brother, the Mayor. The two lovers were Richard Burton and Claire Bloom, both starting on the careers that soon attained stardom. Claire and I shared a dressing-room. She was a beautiful child and very grave, but I managed to infect her with some of my incurable frivolity. In those days she hadn't developed into the enchanting young woman I was to meet again fifteen years later in another of John's productions,

Chekhov's *Ivanov* and most recently of all as Nora in *A Doll's House*—a wonderful performance. Eliot Makeham was the Chaplain, sweet and endearing, and of course Peter Bull's Tappercoom was one of the major performances. Our beloved Esmé Percy, who helped John to direct, was Skipps, the rag-and-bone man. His performance varied every night. Sometimes he would reach unbelievable heights, sometimes he would ramble along according to the mood of the moment, to our consternation but always charming the audience.

John is at his best a brilliant director, but such a perfectionist that he never seems entirely satisfied with the day's work and will arrive at the theatre the morning after we have dutifully marked down our moves, and change them all. I believe he has been known to import a new move at so late a date as the first night. But when you get used to his methods they cease to worry you: for my own part I've stopped writing down my moves when he directs.

After a month of rehearsals we took *The Lady* on a lengthy tour, learning how to play the beautiful but exacting parts Christopher had written for us. At first there seemed so many ways of interpreting a line. At one rehearsal I called out to John, 'I don't know how to say this line!' From the stalls came the stentorian command: 'Say it!' and in some trepidation, I said it.

Our West End run started at the Globe Theatre in May, 1949, and was an enormous success. All through the summer, a particularly hot one, we played to packed houses. We all lost weight under the beautiful dresses designed by Oliver Messel, for the weather was more suited to shall we say *O Calcutta* than the heavy trappings of the fourteenth century. Nevertheless it was a wonderfully happy run. John has the gift of turning his company into a Band of Brothers, though like George Orwell's Big Brother his eye is continually watchful. He and I were devoted crossword solvers. We used to keep a copy of *The Times* in the quick-change room and between scenes would feverishly jot down a word before rushing on for our next entrance.

The Lady ran through the summer and autumn and came to an end the following January. We were booked to open in New York in October; in the meantime we went our several ways. John did a season at Stratford-upon-Avon. It was then that he created his memorable Angelo in *Measure for Measure*. I did some radio and television and in the late spring appeared as the housekeeper in *Rosmersholm* which we toured before coming to the St Martin's Theatre. Michael McOwan directed and Robert Harris played Rosmersholm. Rebecca was in the hands of the Swedish actress, Signe Hasso. She wasn't really suited but she was such a fascinating person you could forgive her shortcomings. The run finished tactfully in time for me to begin rehearsing for the American season of *The Lady*.

There were one or two changes in the cast. Claire's place was taken by Penelope Munday, and George Howe, a good friend of mine, took over from Harcourt Williams. It was almost like starting on a new play. Of course John manoeuvered numerous changes too, but since the lines were the same there wasn't much difficulty in recalling them.

We flew to New York at the beginning of October. It was my first long flight and after a few exciting hours it became quite boring with nothing to look at except sometimes endless stretches of blue sky and sometimes endless flocks of clouds. But coming into Boston at night by air was lovely, looking down on the city with all its lights ablaze. We stayed there for two weeks and were a great success. My chief memory of that time was that we heard of the death of Bernard Shaw and we all felt his loss, though I had never had the honour of meeting him. But I'd been in a good many of his plays—of course *You Never Can Tell* took first place.

Then down we went to New York: after a couple of pre-views we opened at the Royale Theatre in a blaze of glory. At Adrianne Allen's apartment on Park Avenue, we stayed to read the glowing notices early next morning. John of course was adored (he is a sort of god in America) but we had all of us made a success. Later in the season I made the acquaintance of Adrianne's very young daughter, Anna Massey, who, having executed a tap-dance for us that evening, went on to become a celebrated actress.

Of all the many parties showered on us, the one I recall most clearly was given by Margery Maude, Cyril Maude's daughter, because it was there that I met Ruth Draper. After the party we were driven home in a taxi shared by Miss Draper herself, and suddenly she said, 'If you'd not all been so busy talking I'd have given you some of my sketches.' Instantly one of our party ordered the driver to return to the house where doubtless our hostess was enjoying the left-overs, with her feet up. However, she seemed undaunted and we all sat round and listened to Ruth Draper in three or four of her superb sketches. As her only 'prop' she borrowed a black velvet stole I was wearing, now one of my cherished possessions.

As well as the parties there were matinees at other theatres and Sunday concerts at Carnegie Hall. I heard Artur Rubinstein, Clifford Curzon and Solomon. I am grateful to have heard Solomon at his best. And there was Christmas: in New York it seems to start in October when the shops are decorated and you hear the strains of the *Adeste Fideles* while you're choosing underwear in the big stores on Fifth Avenue. And then, a few weeks before Christmas comes Thanksgiving with its glut of traditional turkey.

We could have run well into the next season but for John's London commitments. After closing in New York we visited Philadelphia and Washington, both fascinating cities. In Washington the British Embassy gave us a cocktail party. By that time we'd become accustomed to the warmth of American hospitality, noticeably lacking in our English hosts. They seemed a bit chilly and grand, though I did find some of them friendly enough when visiting their own homes.

I'm fonder of Washington than of any other American city. We were too early in the year for the famous cherry blossom, but the dazzling whiteness of the buildings, the sweep of long avenues, the picture-galleries and perhaps best of all, the Lincoln Memorial, were unforgettable.

Altogether it was an exciting experience, but I was glad to be going home. After a few months in the States I'm always yearning for England. Wandering through the aridities of Central Park in the spring sets me longing for our own parks with their trees and flowering shrubs and clumps of daffodils. The one moment of magic in New York is the evening, when the skyscrapers shine through the red and gold of sunset like fairy palaces. But London is changing year by year, you could almost say day by day. Today you'll drive down a street and to-morrow find it labelled 'One-way'. Our city, built to be horizontal, is receiving something that might be called a face-lift; we are growing rapidly vertical. Sky-scrapers of frightening ugliness tower above lovely little Georgian houses already marked down for demolition. We still have our parks and our trees, but who knows when they too will become sites for office-blocks and we shall be a wilderness of monkeys with no trees to climb.

A year or two before going to New York I had read Elizabeth Myers' novel, *Mrs Christopher*, and thought what a splendid play it would make. I wrote to ask her permission to dramatise it and received a kind and encouraging reply, but before I could go any further Elizabeth Myers died. I got in touch with her husband, Littleton Powys, one of the Powys brothers, and he gave me the go-ahead. I went down to his home in Sherborne several times, when we discussed the play and became great friends. When in New York with *The Lady* I met a man of the theatre who did all he could to get it put on, but without success, and *Mrs Christopher* retired into limbo with my other attempts at playwriting. Between the wars I had also devoted a good deal of time to writing short stories, about which I think I've spoken already. I still have a go at them from time to time, more or less successfully. As well, I've two novels to my credit, or maybe debit, as they are lying by, unpublished. Perhaps there will come a time. Once when I was young and dabbling in that dubious game Planchette, a personage calling himself Oscar Wilde condescended to tell me that the novel I was then trying to write would be published 'After you're a corpse.' Something to look forward to, I suppose.

After I came home from the States I had quite an uneventful year. It wasn't until the autumn of 1951 that I did another West End play, *Indian Summer*, by the late Peter Watling. John directed and I had the part of an unsuccessful proof-reader. During the play she receives a letter of dismissal. The stage-manager had written this so convincingly that I was near to tears every time I read it. Just as well that I didn't have to read it aloud. John, as ever, was wonderfully helpful. He's a master of inflexion. Sometimes I'd go home, fairly satisfied with my own interpretation of a line, and then it would dawn on me that he was right and I was wrong. *Indian Summer* ran, alas, for only three weeks, to our great disappointment as we all believed in the play. Margaret Halstan, whom I'd not met since she played Ophelia at the Vic nearly forty years before, was in the cast.

January brought *Sunset in Knightsbridge*, dramatised by John Ireland Wood from Pamela Hansford Johnson's book, *The Avenue of Stone*. Again a short run but it led to a meeting with John Fernald and the offer of the Nurse in *Uncle Vanya* at the Arts Theatre. I'd already played the part at Oxford, and since then have been in two television versions. I have been in a good many of Chekhov's plays. Each one has a special quality I've not met in any other playwright. Whatever *Sturm und Drang* the characters may be going through, there is a prevailing sense of peace—I can't explain it. It makes one think of gliding down a river or sitting among trees in a silent wood. The very antithesis of Ibsen, who gives you the sensation of battling through a blinding snowstorm. Rather like those nightmares where you are trying to run away and your feet remain anchored to the ground.

I hadn't played at the Arts Theatre before. As far as dressing-rooms are concerned it is terribly congested and it's as well to be on friendly terms with your room-mates, but the theatre itself is charming and usually audiences are warm and responsive. It was while playing in *Uncle Vanya* that I was given the chance of being in H M Tennent's production of Shaw's *The Millionairess*, with Katharine Hepburn as the star. I went down to the Globe Theatre to read the part, that of a sweated East End seamstress, to Katharine and the director, Michael Benthall. Katharine came up from the stalls, a slim figure in a white trouser-suit, and asked whether I'd ever played any Cockney parts, and then, book in hand, I launched on the part and went away, not sure whether I'd passed the test or not. But that afternoon Felix de Wolfe rang me, saying 'We're in!'

Katharine was wonderful to work with. There's magic if you like! There is a warm friendliness about her once you have broken through her initial reserve. In the short scene we had together she was always responsive, never exploiting her own personality, always considerate of yours. I got to know her well and loved her. We went to New York after a run in London at the New Theatre, and spent Christmas there. It is customary to play on Christmas night, but Katharine insisted that we got the night off. She gave us all a present of money, to buy whatever we most wanted. I chose an exquisite little watch, black of face and surrounded by pearls. On the back is engraved, 'Nora from Kate'. I wear it always. She is a faithful friend. When I was in *Forty Years On* and she was in front she came backstage to see me and was as sweet and friendly as ever.

Her performance in *The Millionairess* was masterly. She looked radiant in the gorgeous dresses Balmain had designed for her; even the shabby raincoat and hat she wore in the East End scene didn't detract from her beauty. At the end of the run she gave the company a bumper party at her house in Greenwich Village, and then it was goodbye to her and a most happy engagement.

Back in London I was at the Arts Theatre again in Peter Cotes's production of Strindberg's *The Father*. I considered it an honour to be playing the Nurse to Wilfred Lawson's magnificent Father. On the first night the house rose at him; I've rarely heard such an ovation. He was a genius, with all the eccentricities that seem part of a genius's make-up, but at his best he had very few equals. There again, as with Katharine, was responsiveness and magic.

Just after the run of *The Lady* I had a faint chance of playing the Mother in Christopher Fry's *The Boy with a Cart*, a part I'd always coveted. But it so happened that it was played by Mary Jerrold and I was bound to admit it was perfect casting. However, later on I was offered the part on television and in spite of the strain of playing it 'live' it was a great experience.

Very soon after that I descended from those sublime heights to play in a ridiculous and charming comedy, *Trial and Error*, with Constance Cummings and Naunton Wayne. I was Connie's aunt, a deaf lady whose hearing aid was a complicated contrivance concocted principally out of a pressure-cooker and a variety of strings. I'm very much against making game of deafness which seems to me the worst of all afflictions endured by the elderly (up to date, thank God, I've escaped it) but in this instance the wearer was joyfully attached to her instrument so I don't think it caused offence. After the London run we took the play on tour and finished up in the spring of 1954 when I went straight into another comedy, *The Facts of Life*, with Alec Clunes, Avice Landon and

Iris Hoey. I had known Iris vaguely since my schooldays but hadn't acted with her before.

One of the leading parts in *The Facts of Life* was played by a boy, Lance Secretan, a precocious youth with heaps of talent and even more self-confidence. He lost no time in giving us hints as to how we should play our parts. I've not met him since and don't know what he's doing, but I'd never be surprised to find myself some day being directed in a play or film and like Sweet Alice, trembling with fear at his frown. But my chief memory of *The Facts of Life* is the awful night when I lost my voice. I finished the play completely voiceless but not before reducing us all to hopeless giggles by my struggles to keep going. 'Of course you must go at once to Norman Punt,' said Alec Clunes. So early next morning off I went, to whisper my complaint to Norman. I was sent home with the admonition to keep silent for the next thirty-six hours. Zacharias had my sincere sympathy, but in two days' time my voice and I had returned to the theatre. From that day on, Norman and his family have ranked among my dearest friends. My first meeting with Jonathan, the only son, was during the run of *Listen to the Wind*, where he made a very youthful member of the audience. We became close friends, and even now, when he is married and a fully fledged doctor, I am still 'Aunty Nora'.

I wasn't in love with my part in *The Facts of Life*, that of a Cockney servant, and was relieved when the run finished and I went to New York in Graham Greene's *The Living Room*, a play largely misunderstood, though it had quite a long run in London. Walter Fitzgerald, Michael Goodliffe and I flew over to rehearse with Hugh Hunt, who was directing, much to my satisfaction. The rest of the cast were English, with the exception of Barbara Bel Geddes, playing Rose, and Ann Shoemaker, the younger of the two sisters. The weather was humid and enervating, and by the time we opened in Newhaven, home of so many English try-outs, we were fairly exhausted. I played Teresa, the part created by Mary Jerrold. I was able to wear the dresses she wore in the London production, though I can't pretend to have inherited the beauty of her performance. Since her death I have played many parts which should have been hers had she lived and I always regard her as an example of perfect acting.

After successful weeks at Newhaven and Boston we came to the Henry Miller Theatre in New York where we were an undeniable flop. Three weeks and we were bound for home. I think the New Yorkers were confused by the apparent anti-Catholic spirit of the play, but I am sure Graham Greene wasn't really out to denigrate his Faith; he was simply emphasising a certain approach to Catholicism by a certain type of Catholic. For myself, I couldn't understand the character of the Priest, so yearning to help, yet so inarticulate, and the fantastic superstition of the two sisters was beyond belief.

While in New York I was seriously contemplating the possibility of being received into the Catholic Church. In a vague sort of way I'd been drawn towards it all my life, but in spite of the fact that so many of my relatives were Catholics, and Constance and most of her children became converts, I remained unconvinced. Ever since leaving school I had undergone various changes of belief, as I've mentioned already. At last, largely through the influence and example of my niece, Veronica Silver, and the three Blakelocks, I more or less promised to receive instruction on my return from the States. Denys Blakelock and I used to have long discussions about religion and I think he was shocked by my apparent indifference. He said to me once, 'You're certainly far from being a Catholic; I'm not sure that you're even a Christian.' He was right. Perhaps it was through that reproachful remark that I began to reconsider my religious attitude or rather, lack of it. On my return from New York Denys introduced me to Father Richard Mangan at the Jesuit Church in Farm

Street where Denys himself had been received many years before. Father Mangan was an inspiring teacher and later became one of my dearest friends. My father had long ago instructed me in many of the doctrines shared by Anglicans and Catholics alike, so I hadn't many difficulties there. But all through my instruction I was slow and distrustful and couldn't make up my mind. Father Mangan, bless his heart, was marvellously patient and just let me take my time. 'Come when you're ready,' he said. 'We're not scalp-hunters.' And at last the day arrived. I was received at Farm Street on the 23rd August, 1955, and had the privilege of being confirmed by Archbishop Roberts, S. J. I had looked forward with dread to my first Confession, but Father Mangan was so understanding that I didn't die of shame as I'd almost expected to do. One of the many things for which I'm thankful to the Church is the help it gave me during the strain and grief of Elaine's illness and death in the summer of that year.

A short while ago I was called upon to speak about the influence of the Catholic Church on the theatre. I think this is far greater than is generally believed. For one thing, non-Catholics have a firm if superstitious belief in the efficacy of our prayers. 'My wife is going for an audition: please pray for her.' 'When you're at Mass do remember my first night.' Moreover, they expect you to be in constant practice. You speak of taking a Sunday in the country. 'How will you fit in Mass?' asks a friend who has no intention of going himself. You make a disparaging remark about someone, and somebody noted for a biting wit murmurs reproachfully, 'And you a Catholic!'

Speaking in a larger sense, of Catholic influence on the theatre as a whole, I have been inclined, in common with so many of us, to look upon the plays and films of today as being subversive in their message owing to the absence of restriction. The other day I was discussing this with a playwright friend of mine and he opened my eyes to another view. These plays which we think we ought to deplore are rarely written with any immoral or licentious intention. In many instances they are simply the outcome of a desire to cleanse the human outlook, to eliminate pretence and false values. In trying to get rid of the somewhat stuffy atmosphere and sometimes hidden innuendo of the so-called drawing-room comedy, their conception of arriving at the truth may be more of the naked truth than appeals to many of us, but don't let us be too swift in condemning these writers. We might try to arrive at a better understanding of their ideals. I'm not suggesting that we should hurl ourselves regardless into this type of play. For myself, obviously the problem doesn't arise, but I do feel that unless a play contains a definitely destructive message, it shouldn't be condemned out of hand.

In the twenties and thirties plays in the West End were mostly comedies, and light comedies at that. Except for a few pieces like *Journey's End*, the theatre wore rather a frivolous dress. Perhaps it was a natural reaction. After the Second World War the fashion changed; playwrights took a more serious attitude, and though comedies were still popular, they often had an underlying stratum of pathos and even tragedy. The 'Kitchen Sink' type of drama had its long day; since its waning there has risen a growing influx of plays in which regular plot is subordinate to the complex workings of the human mind. All these developments may again be a natural reaction. At the present time the disturbed state of the world is influencing thought in so many directions and notably in the theatre. The two religious plays dealing with the life of Christ, *Godspell* and *Jesus Christ, Superstar*, are drawing huge audiences. Of course a certain percentage may be attracted simply by an appetite for something new in the theatre, but on the occasions when I saw each of these plays, the audience was largely composed of young people obviously spellbound. Many of these may have reached adolescence without any real knowledge of the Gospels and the life of Christ; spirited and entertaining as these plays are on the surface, they could be the means of encouraging young audiences to look into spiritual things for the first time. They may be the cause of a religious renaissance. Drugs and 'porn' can lose their attraction—here might be something lasting.

Each of these plays has a different approach: *Godspell*, simple, gay and deeply moving, is to my mind by far the more appealing. *Superstar*, in my opinion, laid so much stress on the material, that often the spiritual was sadly lacking, but even so, there was something to learn if you looked for it. The theatre, in all its aspects, is bound to influence us for good or ill. But, as Shakespeare, man of the theatre, tells us: 'Heaven is above all yet.'

I will conclude this chapter by another quotation; this time a free translation from Saint Augustine: 'Love God and do as you like.' It sounds contradictory, doesn't it, but on analysis it becomes the simplest advice. If you love God you are necessarily doing as you like, because when you love someone, what *you* like is what *he* likes.

X

LADIES OF THE SCREEN

When Elaine died in the summer of 1955 I was working in television, always anxious about what might be happening in my absence, though she was looked after by a magnificent nurse. But mercifully I was with her when she died, early in July. Perhaps the stars were against some of us just then. So many of my friends were going through a difficult time. It spread even to the most exalted of us: Princess Margaret's brave decision about her marriage affected the whole nation. Politics or no, I'm a Royalist at heart. But my grief came before everything. The Chelsea flat, bereft of Elaine's presence, was no longer a home; even Chelsea itself seemed alien and I lost no time in moving. I found a flat in Earls Court Square where I lived for the next six years. The flat was on the first floor of a large, converted house. Looking back I can't think why it attracted me so much. Its high ceilings and imposing French windows I found alluring. I had it decorated in a flamboyant style that wouldn't have any appeal for me now. Just then I wanted space and vivid colours. Now I'm all for white walls and simplicity, even my taste in clothes has gone pastel. During my tenancy I suffered a burglary which may have had something to do with my gradual dislike of the flat.

I'd barely made the move from Chelsea before becoming immersed in the film, *A Town Like Alice*, which kept me at Pinewood studios from August until late November. There is no need for me to expatiate on the story of the film—Nevil Shute's book is too well known for that. It made a magnificent film which to this day is revived from time to time and never fails to reduce me to floods of tears, though in the actual shooting there was plenty of laughter and fun. Jack Lee, the director, something of a martinet, soon endeared himself to us. Marie Löhr, Jean Anderson, Renée Houston and Virginia McKenna gave grand performances and we all became inseparable. Beforehand we had all been admonished to keep our weight down and get as sun-burnt as possible. I had no difficulty in conforming to the first of these rules: the long strain of Elaine's illness had made me as thin as a pencil. We wore the minimum of clothes; as time went on my own dress was split from stem to stern; which was all right during the sweltering summer days: but autumn found us shivering and prone to colds and 'flu. Much of the actual shooting in Malaya was done before we ourselves started; they were chiefly long shots with deputies approximating to our shape and size. The intimate scenes were then shot on location at Burnham Beeches, where there was a horrid swampy expanse of water through which we waded knee-deep, to emerge steeped in mud and thankful for the hot drinks and nips of brandy provided by the management. Marie Löhr heroically lent me a pair of combinations that had belonged to her mother, Kate Bishop, which I'm sure helped to save me from pneumonia. There was one scene in which the hero, Peter Finch, was threatened with crucifixion: we shot it on a dim September night with a blanket of rain dripping down on our scantily-clothed bodies. 'More sweat, more mud', was Jack Lee's constant command to the make-up girls. There was a solitary sequence when, released from imprisonment, we were actually clean and reasonably respectable, which was blissful. I played a hypochondriac who resorted almost continuously to remedies for her imaginary ills.

The last day at Pinewood was a real dramatic climax. We were involved in a realistic rainstorm: water cascading down from the overhead mechanism. We'd been advised to bring a change of underwear as we might get rather wet. This proved to be the understatement *in excelsis*. By the end of the day we were drenched to the skin, our perfunctory dresses clinging like limpets to our freezing bodies. This was especially disconcerting for me as I was due that evening at the Arts Theatre for my first rehearsal of a children's play, and incidentally my first meeting with the director, the young Peter Hall. I flung myself into a bath, rushed to hairdressing to implore them to do something with my hair, threw on a rational make-up and drove breakneck to the theatre. Peter Hall hadn't yet come into his own. He had all the potentialities of a splendid director; his authority was compelling even in those days. He was known as 'The Baby Genius'. Years later when he had made his name, I reminded him of the title. 'Well, at any rate, not *baby* any more', was his modest response!

The children's play, *Listen to the Wind*, with enchanting music by Vivian Ellis, was pure enjoyment. I played the fantastic grandmother of a trio of children who mercifully suffered from none of those 'taught' voices and mannerisms common to so many child-actors. Having completely lost my singing voice I was allowed to speak my numbers to the music.

Miriam Karlin, whose work is so well-known in films, television and theatre, played a mermaid named Miranda and had some entertaining scenes. She and I shared a dressing-room and got on remarkably well, so that it surprised us when we were told that someone in the audience had said, 'It's easy to see Miriam Karlin and Nora Nicholson don't get on.' The fact that we sedulously avoided one another's eyes for fear of 'corpsing' must have occasioned this acid comment.

After a brief holiday in Cornwall I went on tour with Dulcie Gray and Michael Denison in Dulcie's own play, *Love Affair*. I felt I was miscast and wasn't very happy, although I enjoyed a warm friendship with Michael and Dulcie. I was glad when, at the end of the tour, came the offer of a part in T S Eliot's *Family Reunion*. Peter Brook directed this with a cast headed by Sybil, Lewis, Paul Scofield and Gwen Frangcon-Davies. For all his cherubic

appearance and soft voice, Peter was quite a disciplinarian and the rehearsals at the Phoenix Theatre were
herculean. It was an ordeal to open 'cold' and on the
first night I was eaten up with nerves. But it was a
wonderful play to be in. We were captivated by Eliot's
beautiful language and soon forgot our nerves. We had a
limited run of about twelve weeks. One night Eliot
came up on the stage and talked to us. My memory of
him is of a gentle personality unexpected from the writer
of such electric poetry.

Those two poet-playwrights, T S Eliot and Christopher
Fry, how different they are both in appearance and their
approach. Eliot seemed essentially serious. I have acted
in only one of his plays and am not too well acquainted
with the rest, but I haven't been able to discover a sense
of humour. Christopher's work abounds in humour and
his face is alive with it; his characters, however deep their
susceptibilities, are never far from laughter. Perhaps
Eliot's rhythm is easier to speak than Christopher's
which rockets away in a kaleidoscope of imagery, but
they are both most satisfying playwrights.

After the run of *Family Reunion* I was in various television plays directed by Peter Potter who had done *The
Facts of Life*. He employed so many of the same people
that we regarded ourselves as a sort of repertory company. He never cast me to type; I was burnt at the stake
in Masefield's *The Witch*, and took to a sick bed as a
nonogenarian in a beautiful play by Susan Pearson,
called *Close My Door*. It was really ahead of its time and
didn't have the acclaim it deserved. If it were revived
I'm sure it would be a success, and as for me, I'm a little
nearer the right age.

In common with most other actresses, from time to
time I am sent the script of a play to read. One in
particular comes to mind. It was in the early days of the
'Kitchen Sink' period which was flourishing at the Royal
Court Theatre. The play was John Arden's *Live Like
Pigs*, and the part suggested for me an ancient hag whose

name I've forgotten but it was something like Old Beastly. Just my cup of tea, I thought, as I settled down to read it. But I'd not pursued further than the first two pages before I decided it wasn't anything like my cup. In those early days of avant garde theatre, you didn't have to be definitely a 'square' to find them difficult to appreciate. Anyway I decided against it. It was revived only the other day. I didn't see it but I'm pretty sure it was regarded as fairly *vieux jeu*, compared with the majority of plays currently in the West End. I don't think there has ever been so rapid a change in theatre-going taste as in the last ten, or even five years. Even I, Old Square that I am, can now watch with enjoyment plays that in the late fifties and early sixties I would have revolted from. Perhaps one must revert to Restoration times fully to appreciate their idiom.

I paid another visit to Toronto after a lapse of more than twenty years, this time in the television version of *Corinth House*. Toronto seemed to me much the same as it was, except for the imposing television studios which of course were non-existent in 1932. My circumstances too were different. Instead of playing small parts with the added indignity of travelling with a false photograph, I was starring in a wonderful part. I was much impressed by the rehearsal rooms, fitted with all essential props and furniture, but when it came to transmission, the dressing-room accommodation turned out to be deplorable—just one room for all the women. As I was, as usual, abysmally nervous I longed for a little privacy, but the show turned out a success. It was of course done 'live'; recorded performances were still years ahead. Some actors maintain that a live performance has an electric quality lacking in a recorded one. I disagree. You are just as anxious, just as much on your toes, even when you know that a fluff or even a dry can be remedied.

And then Veronica and I took a holiday in Vienna, one of the highlights of all my holidays. Vienna is surely one of the most glamorous cities in the world. The

C.D.—I

people are so friendly, you are given a '*Gruss Gott*' wherever you go, and your halting German seems no handicap. I found it quite easy to fall into the language, even though it was a lifetime since Saarbrücken. We lived under the spell of almost nightly visits to the Opera; Tito Gobbi and Schwarzkopf in *Falstaff,* and Hilde Borkh as an unforgettable Electra. The enthusiasm of the audiences was marvellous. The King and Queen of Greece were present at *Electra,* and I've never heard such applause, their majesties joining in with the best of them. This was my second encounter with the King and Queen. They had been present at a performance of *Family Reunion* and had come up on the stage afterwards.

Then we had a magic morning at the Spanish Riding-School, visits to Schönbrunn, numberless picture-galleries and churches, and of course we sampled any amount of restaurants. Our hotel was cheap so we went all out on food. There was Demels, famous for exotic cakes, and one night we dined at the celebrated Sachers. We got ourselves up in our very best, and then I went and ruined it all. I had tucked my table-napkin in my waist-belt. It wasn't until we had sailed out of the dining-room, feeling like duchesses, that I became conscious of my unglamorous white apron. I didn't dare go back, so to this day the Sacher napkin is in my possession. A souvenir? Or should it be regarded as a theft?

I can't make up my mind whether I'd rather spend my last years in Vienna or Killarney. Perhaps Killarney, being in my beloved Ireland. I once had a week there and it lived up to its reputation for beauty. Even those picture postcards we never quite credit aren't an exaggeration of the glowing colours of its mountains and lakes. I used to go on expeditions in coaches and perilous jaunting cars; Muckross Abbey, Glengariff, and a wonderful hour in Dingle Bay to watch the blessing of the boats. An obscure touring company was giving performances in Killarney—I saw two of these and had the doubtful privilege of watching some of the worst acting in my experience. But even this couldn't spoil the holiday and the sun shone all the time.

I had first met Thora Hird while filming *Fools Rush In*, in 1948, but we didn't work together again for another ten years or so, when we went on a tour of Gerald Savory's play, *So Many Children*. She and I and Arthur Lowe, later to be celebrated in *Dad's Army*, were a North-country trio: Thora and Arthur two lovable characters and myself a really villainous creature with a sweetly deceptive exterior. All through the tour we were banking on coming into London. The play, full of comedy and pathos, deserved a West End run, but brought us no nearer than Golders Green where the bus-strike successfully kept us from continuing. Since then we have done the play twice on television and still entertain a lingering hope that some day we shall give London the pleasure of our company.

Another play which didn't catch on was James Parrish's *The Woman on the Stair* directed by Jack Minster. I had made friends with him long ago on Barry Jackson's Canadian Tour. He was a long-faced person who seldom smiled but had a delicious, sardonic sense of humour, for which he was affectionately known in the profession as 'Jolly Jack'. It was pleasant to be directed by him though the play ran for only twelve nights. Gwen Watford starred as a blind girl who is the means of discovering a murder and I was the victim; we had a two-level set and it fell to my lot to be perched on the higher level, so being subject to a horror of heights, I wasn't too happy and wasn't sorry when the murderer came along and finished me off. Later on I played the same part in a television version with Flora Robson as the blind woman. While lying on the floor and being discovered by Flora, I was seized with an irrepressible desire to swallow. 'They'll be concentrating on Flora,' thought I, 'and not noticing me', so I felt safe and swallowed. In one of the papers the following day, came the remark: 'The corpse was seen to swallow decorously.'

Having recovered from the Westminster play and a bout of 'flu, I embarked on one of the happiest engagements of my career in Noël Coward's *Waiting in the Wings*. It was the story of a group of elderly actresses living in retirement in a house reminiscent of Ivor Novello's 'Redroofs'. I was a slightly demented lady named Serita Myrtle, a big star in her far-off day. She lived entirely in her romantic past, so much so that all through the run I never felt conscious of my advanced age: I was a perpetual twenty-three. After nearly setting the house on fire through an innocent passion for throwing away lighted matches, the authorities dispatched her to a more secluded home. She was delighted to go. Just another theatrical job; and she left her colleagues without a qualm.

Peggy Webster directed the play in which Sybil and Marie Löhr were the leads, and Lewis Casson an old man still in love with an actress aged ninety who lived somewhere upstairs and never appeared. He visited her every day, bearing a bunch of violets; an extremely touching performance.

Noël Coward came to only one rehearsal, our last before flying to Dublin for the opening. Most of the cast were old friends of his. I had never met him and was dreading the prospect of rehearsing with 'The Master' in front. Before rehearsal started I was sitting at the side of the stage, when in burst our author, seized my hand and exclaimed, 'I'm so glad you're in this,' to which, somewhat shaken, I replied, 'I hope you'll go on being glad' and edged away to allow his chums to gather round him with endearing cries.

The rehearsal passed off smoothly. Noël came up on the stage. I remained in the background, conscious of being a stranger. He approached me and my heart sank in apprehension, and then leapt to an unbelievable height at his one word: 'Impeccable!' It had never been said to me before and doubtless will never be said again so I do hope I may be forgiven for mentioning it.

In the cast most of us were 'oldies' and had often worked together before. But we were dogged by a series of misfortunes. Two of the company died during the run and ensuing tour. One was Maureen Delaney, an old Irish actress whom we all loved. I used to call on her in the dressing-room every night and ask, 'How are you?' to which she invariably answered, 'Lovely, darling.' She doled me out drops of Holy Water into an aspirin bottle. The Holy Water has long since blest its last, but I cherish the little bottle. Among lesser calamities, many of us suffered from accidents. On the first night Marie Löhr fractured her arm and heroically went on to give a fine performance, her arm in a sling. She said the pain kept her from feeling nervous. The accident occurred just before the show. Coming down the steps of St Martin-in-the-Fields where she had been offering up a prayer for our success, she slipped, it being a particularly wet night. Said Noël Coward, 'Couldn't she have chosen a church without any steps?'

Perhaps the superstitious would attribute those sad events to the fact that the play contained a quotation from *Macbeth*, which as every professional knows, is taboo. It fell to my lot to speak the line ('Out damned spot!') and I often wondered whether anyone else considered its impact. But I can't believe that so glorious a play could bring ill-luck, though I have heard that the actual lines spoken by the Witches are laced with black magic. When I was playing one of the Witches at Oxford, we used to say the Our Father before the Cauldron Scene, to ward off evil spirits. In any case, whatever the play, a swift prayer before one's first entrance is to my mind essential.

Later on in 1961 I did a television adaptation of a book called *Mrs Ross* by Ronald Nicolson. The play was called *The Whisperers*. I had a magnificent part, an old woman living in her own fantasy-world. I was dis-

131

appointed when a few years later it was filmed and the part played by Edith Evans. I'd have been still more disappointed had anyone else been cast for it, but you simply can't be jealous of such a superb artist. Very soon after this the profession went through a bad patch, owing to the Equity Strike which stopped our performing on ITV. I plunged into writing the novels I've talked of already. The agent who handled them had great hopes, but after many fruitless visits to publishers they made their sorrowful home-coming.

I think it was in the spring of 1962 that I was again at the Lyric, Hammersmith, in a Russian play, *Come Back With Diamonds*, which began and finished almost without time for us to take a breath. I've very little recollection of the plot but I rather enjoyed myself as the hero's mother. In the last act I was supposed to be paralysed and sat on the raked stage in a wheel-chair, saying nothing but looking volumes! I found the play important chiefly for the performance of a young understudy who went on for a leading part at practically a moment's notice. A memorable performance, though Glenda Jackson, then completely unknown, has probably forgotten all about it. Now she is a star, but to me that first success is something to remember.

During the summer I left Earls Court for Chelsea, my spiritual home, once more. High up in a block of flats in the King's Road, I lived in a flurry of traffic and had the benefit of studying the most trendy fashions. You picked your way about the crowded street, stiff with antique-shops and boutiques exhibiting the latest craze of Young Chelsea. That was Chelsea in the early sixties; today of course it is notorious and Carnaby Street pales beside it. I find some of these youngsters quite endearing with their flamboyant attire and flowing hair, though often you are hard put to it to decide on their sex. Nowadays there is nothing unusual in my own men-friends' extravagant dress. I find multi-coloured suits, brilliant ties and lace-embroidered evening shirts quite an attractive change from the sober dress of the young men of my youth. Particularly the evening dress of that period: tail-coats, boiled shirts, stiff, upstanding collars—their wearers were often constrained to bring a spare to change into half-way through an evening's dancing—and of course no man could go gloveless to a dance.

The agent to whom I'd submitted my novels made me an interesting proposition. Would I like to write a life of Alma Taylor? I don't suppose the name Alma Taylor rings even the faintest bell in the ears of this generation. In the twenties she was perhaps the most popular of all British film stars. I was her ardent fan and still remember *Comin' thro' the Rye*, her biggest success. I jumped at the idea of trying to write her life. I felt that my only way of attempting it would be to write in the first person, subject to Miss Taylor's approval, get her to give me personal interviews, take notes and steep myself so much in her personality as to make it my own. She agreed and there began a series of sessions at Alma's house in Wandsworth, where she has lived since her retirement and widowhood some years ago. She is a perfectly enchanting person, and would talk while I took copious notes and had access to multitudes of photographs, press-cuttings and her own personal reminiscences.

I wrote one chapter, dealing with her early years and first appearances on the screen as a child-actress. She had gone into the film business innocently and thought her audition was a sort of party. Alma was so responsive that I really began to feel an inner transformation, as if I'd really taken on her personality. But as I got more deeply involved I found it all increasingly difficult. By nature Alma Taylor was so unassuming that it was hard to give her story the dramatic quality expected when depicting the life of a film star. Also just then I was working pretty hard at my own job and couldn't give the time necessary for so formidable a task. So regretfully I threw in my hand: cowardly perhaps, but it was really and truly lack of ability. Alma was very understanding and we both hoped someone more suited would carry on the work. Nothing has come of it so far, but I feel many people would love to read a really authentic biography of such a gifted actress.

I have already written about London's Little Theatres which were such a flourishing concern between the wars and have now taken on fresh activity. One of the most successful is the Hampstead Theatre Club which has several West End transfers to its credit. Early in 1964, James Roose-Evans, founder and at that time director, put on a play by an Australian writer, Hal Porter, called *The Tower*. It concerned that part of Australia known in the last century as Van Diemen's Land, and was a most interesting treatment of the still existing slavery problem. Sebastian Shaw and I played opposite each other; the first time we had acted together since the production of *Rope*. The play was couched in an idiom strange to us and was difficult to learn, but all the same I thought it should have had a transfer and would stand a revival now.

Playing at the tiny Hampstead Theatre was something of a strain. With four of us dressing in close proximity and vast crinolines, and the consciousness that anything you said above a whisper was liable to travel to the auditorium, the atmosphere was to say the least, cramping. Another drawback was that in this particular production there was no curtain, so that before the beginning of each act, in spite of a hollow voice announcing that the curtain would rise in five minutes, it did nothing of the kind, and you, if unlucky enough to open the act, had to walk boldly on to the stage and wait for the house lights to dim. And as you and the audience were on bowing terms, this was quite upsetting. One night an undisciplined gentleman, evidently recognising me, called out, 'Hullo, love.' Friendly, if inappropriate to the action of the play. Every night I used to make my first entrance, sick with nerves and trusting I wouldn't catch the eye of anyone I might know in the audience.

XI

TELEUIJION JAGA

It was a relief and also a great joy to be working again with John Gielgud in his production of *Ivanov* at the Phoenix Theatre in the summer of 1965, after a bout of radio and television. *Ivanov*, one of Chekhov's early plays, is not up to the standard of his later work, but it has much of that peculiar beauty that only he can create. Rehearsals proceeded according to John's invariable pattern: changes, changes all the way, but by this time I was used to all that, except that I was never quite sure how he wanted me to play my part, that of a marriage-broker, an eccentric woman named Avdotva Nazatovna. So all through rehearsals I was in a somewhat feverish state of mind. I didn't feel really at home in the part until we'd been running for some weeks. John had given me a bit of business that I simply couldn't do. On the first night, just after a protracted dress-rehearsal which came to an end only because the curtain was shortly due to rise, I approached John in despair. John, encumbered as he was with the production and his own exacting part, took me aside and went through the little scene with me. I quote this merely to show how infinitely considerate and unselfish he is. When it came to the scene, I'm ashamed to say, whether owing to nerves or more likely complete inability, I muffed the bit of business and for the rest of the run it stayed as it was in the beginning. Not a word of reproach from John; perhaps he didn't notice. Perhaps he thought, 'Poor Nora, she just can't do it.'

Ivanov had a limited run before it was taken to the States where it was only a moderate success. There were several changes of cast. Yvonne Mitchell's part of Ivanov's wife was played by Vivien Leigh, one of her last appearances before her tragic death. Ethel Griffies took over from me. I've known her for many years; a marvellous example of the ability to remain a successful actress when aged over ninety. Before the play went to New York we did two shows on television, one in black and white for the United Kingdom, the other in colour for America. Colour, then in its infancy, was even then very successful, I thought.

The day of the second transmission was memorable for me. After two days' intensive work in the studio under fierce lights, I was whisked off in a car to travel through the night to the heart of Devonshire for location work on a television play by James Hanley, *A Walk in the Sea*. I arrived at the village of Branscombe somewhere around midnight after a journey of about four hours, fell into bed in the extremely comfortable hotel, and was up betimes on the morrow, made up and ready for work. I managed to survive. It was a beautiful play in which a talented black cat and I were co-stars. He was one of the most co-operative artists I've ever worked with. Viewers may remember the tragic ending to the story. After being evicted from her home the woman goes down to the sea and drowns with the cat in her arms. It was mid-winter, very cold and blustery. The cat who had never been to the sea before, took the experience with complete *sang froid*. I was mercifully spared the ordeal of that walk into the sea. I had a stand-in who was supposed to be of my build and height. Actually it was a young man, an ex-jockey, I believe. My doctor, talking to me about that scene, remarked, 'I thought your ankles looked a bit puffy.' I daresay they did.

I have often, both in films and television, played opposite talented animals, but not all of them have been lovable. In *Thomasina*, which starred the small Karen Dotrice, there was a scene in a vet's surgery. The character I played brought her beloved dog—a large person of the spaniel species—to be examined. He lay stretched on my lap while I awaited my turn. He was aged and remarkably smelly. I don't think he ought to have been engaged, for he was literally on his last legs; in fact, I believe he had barely finished the film before he received, so to speak, his cards. I wondered what he had to say about me when he reached the Elysian fields ('Horrible old woman and she smelt awful!') But nearly all my animal-artists have been fragrant and friendly.

It was during the run of *Ivanov* that my sister Angela died after a short illness. Although we didn't meet very often we corresponded weekly and her loss was a great grief to me. Now I am the only one left of my own generation. My two close relatives are my nieces, Antonia and Veronica. Antonia works in an Anglo-Catholic Convent, looking after old people. Her patience is inexhaustible: I wonder where she gets it from, certainly not from my side of the family!

Before coming to take up work in London, Veronica lived in Cambridge, where I often stayed with her. She was the owner of an evil little motor-bike called Ducky, my distrust of which I tried to overcome by taking one unforgettable ride, being a believer in trying everything once. We fled up and down the crowded streets of Cambridge, my heart in my mouth and my arms desperately clasping the intrepid Veronica. I was reminded of the time I'd ridden a tricycle in a film I made in 1954 with Kenneth More called *Raising a Riot*. This monster had a life all its own and no notion of discipline. By the time the film was finished I was the possessor of the most spectacular but necessarily un-manifestable bruises.

In the early part of 1966 my agent rang me to say I'd been offered a part in a new BBC television series of Galsworthy's *The Forsyte Saga*. The part was Juley, one of the Forsyte aunts. The series was to start in May and I was to appear in about ten of the twenty-six episodes. For the moment I hesitated. I had never played in so protracted a series and six months seemed a long period without the possibility of doing anything else. But fortunately for me I soon came to a different conclusion.

137

Donald Wilson, the producer, had adapted the book, and David Giles, with whom I'd worked at the Lyric, Hammersmith, was to direct. So it was settled. Before any shooting began I was subjected to interminable sessions at Nathan's, choosing my dresses. As I am small I was able to wear some contemporary things, beautiful but fragile with age. I used to wonder about the identity of the original wearers and think how surprised they'd be to see their usurper. The period of the series ranged from 1886 or thereabouts until the 1920s, but the old aunts had died long before that. Fay Compton and Nora Swinburne were my two sisters. I knew Nora very well but I'd not acted with Fay and had met her only very occasionally. I was a little apprehensive about acting with her but she turned out to be perfectly delightful, both as an actress (I knew that of course) and a companion. In fact that applied to the whole cast. Several of them I knew already, notably Kenneth More whom I'd last met in *Raising a Riot*. He was Young Jolyon. I think he wasn't quite young enough for the first few episodes, but as the series went on he settled down to give a fine performance. But they were all so good. I can't begin to enumerate them and there is really no need; the *Saga* has become part of our national life and is the passport to so many friends, acquaintances and most of all, perhaps, to the man in the street. Bus-conductors, taxi-drivers, casual passers-by, greet you as an intimate, and that doesn't confine itself to this country. In Ireland, Denmark, Holland, Germany you are often stopped in the street. Even the Church gives you a greeting. Once, going in to Mass, I met one of the priests on his way out. He stopped me saying, 'I'm so sorry you died.' 'Oh, yes,' I replied, 'I died when I was ninety-one.' If any of the departing congregation overheard that remark it must have bewildered them.

I think it was the episode where I, as Aunt Juley, rescued a little dog in the Park and brought it home, to the consternation of Aunt Ann, that really endeared the character to audiences. I've often proved the truth of that adage which maintains that animals steal any show in which they appear. This particular actor certainly dominated the scene where Aunt Juley claims ownership in defiance of her sister. The stern reproach in Fay's voice as she said, 'But the dog will have *followers*!', was enough to intimidate anyone but the besotted Aunt Juley. But I feel that her habit of giving voice to the most naïvely tactless remarks had the effect of making her rather endearing. One of her more embarrassing questions was put to Soames just after the divorce: 'They tell me you have a charming house . . . do you ever hear anything of Irene nowadays?' The family try to shut her up and Soames makes a precipitate exit. Aunt Juley isn't the least disgruntled. Is she really as innocent as we think?

As Soames, Eric Porter gave the performance of his career. The subtlety of his increasing age, in itself a masterpiece of make-up (I believe it took more than an hour to complete) and the way he gradually enlisted the sympathy of the audience was remarkable. A man totally lacking charm, yet Soames contrived to win them over and completely wrest their sympathy from Irene.

Ever since I read *The Man of Property* nearly half a century ago, I've detested the character of Irene. I believe she is supposed to be drawn from life. Certainly Galsworthy painted the most convincing portrait of this woman, who throughout the book is seen merely through the eyes of others; her thoughts, her attitude to life are never expressed personally. To my mind she is the embodiment of selfishness and utter disregard for the feelings of others. Fleur, whose life she did her best to ruin, from purely unselfish motives we are told, is herself a go-getter, but somewhere hidden away beneath that brittle exterior, is a heart, whereas I don't believe Irene's heart beat for anyone save herself. With broken hearts lying all round her, did she care? I don't think I've ever disliked anyone in real life as I dislike the fictional Irene. Even Nyree Dawn Porter's beauty and grace could make no change in my feelings.

Margaret Tyzack (who played Winifred, victim of a disastrous marriage) is in my opinion destined to be one of the finest actresses of her generation. She, like Eric, aged beautifully. Of course she couldn't disguise her youthful contours but her voice, movements and general demeanour were in perfect harmony with her advancing years.

We all loved our director, David Giles. I don't remember any angry words during the whole of the six months I was in the series. We rehearsed in one of those dreary Drill Halls that the BBC used to be so adept at picking out before the new and splendid rehearsal-rooms were opened at North Acton. A 'one-armed bandit' in an adjoining room provided light entertainment between scenes, and a good many of us were crossword addicts. Eric and I would discuss religion and Shakespeare; on the latter subject perhaps we were in better agreement than the first.

In the autumn I had a couple of free weeks and glee-fully went off to Cardiff to do a short television play. Madness, said my friends, but it was a bit of a change and I enjoyed it, especially as the director was June Wyndham-Davies. Back again to the *Saga* until December, when I bade a regretful goodbye to the Forsyte family.

The series came to an end the following May; the final episode was completed just in time to be shown on the air that night. The management gave a party for the entire company. Actors, directors, floor-managers, camera-crew, make-up and wardrobe departments, we were all there. There must have been at least a hundred of the family alone. Many of the actors I had not met before because they had joined the cast after the death of the old generation and a twenty years' gap in the story. I hope that exciting last-night reunion won't be the final meeting of that splendid Fellowship of Players.

I spent the greater part of the spring and summer of 1967 in radio and television. One outstanding television play was another by James Hanley, *That Woman*, which was done 'live'. I had got accustomed to recordings and found this frightening, as we were a cast of only four, and I, as the Woman, was never off the set. Strangely enough it turned out to be one of the most successful plays of my career.

Late in the summer I was fairly exhausted and managed to put in a couple of weeks' holiday in Galway, a sweet and picturesque little town, with Salthill, opposite the bay, not far off, and Connemara within easy distance. I made several expeditions, visited the ancient Abbey of Ballintubber, where daily Mass has been celebrated almost without a break for seven hundred years, and Westport, the home of Lord Sligo, with its collection of pictures and Waterford glass.

I came home to start on a film that kept me going until December. It was an eccentric comedy called *Diamonds for Breakfast*, about an exiled Russian Grand Duke, played by Marcello Mastroianni. I was his aunt, and a Russian lady, Madame Schouvaloff, used to try to acquaint me with the intricacies of a Russian accent. I achieved something not absolutely English but I couldn't pretend it was Russian. For the part I wore some odd garments and one beautiful dress, the copy of one worn by an actual Russian Grand Duchess, in which I quite fancied myself. However, it was seen for only about two minutes' screening time and my vanity suffered an eclipse. We did most of the filming in a disused house in Addison Road, littered with furniture and very uncomfortable, but I enjoyed most of it, chiefly owing to Chris Morahan, who directed. He is elusive and unpredictable but very exciting to work with. I never really got the hang of the story, and remained mystified even when I saw the trade show.

After a few weeks we left Addison Road for Blenheim Palace, in complete and most impressive contrast. One of the scenes was in the library, an imposing room lined with expensively upholstered books protected by glass doors from prying fingers, and, I imagine, readers as well. Most of the cast dressed together, higgledy-piggledy, but Marcello had practically a royal dressing-room—the actual room where Winston Churchill was born. After a spell at Blenheim and a scene in a night-club we wound up in the underground passages of Cliveden. Altogether an odd but interesting engagement.

Filming can be pretty alarming: a strange medium, its sequences are often a series of *non sequiturs*. Halfway through a picture you may find yourself walking down the aisle on the arm of the bridegroom whose death you've been mourning on your first day in the studio. When at last you watch the finished product you marvel how everything has fitted into its proper place. In the theatre the slow rise of the curtain can be disturbing; more so the green light that heralds your first line in a broadcast; even worse, the floor-manager's signal on television, like a wave of farewell. But nothing can be more agonising than the moment when the word 'Action!' means that the executioner's axe has descended. The fact that the skies won't fall if there are two or even half-a-dozen 'takes' of a scene presents no solace. And anyway the first take is often your best.

In television, though you miss the immediate response of a theatre audience, the friendly presence of the crew, the floor-manager and even the director, remote in the control-room, gives an intimate feeling. And as I've said already, the recognition you get from complete strangers can be very heartening. The postman, looking in on you the morning after you've been murdered, says, 'Oh, you're still alive, then?' But you don't always get the reaction you expect. One day, sitting beside a woman in a bus, I received a friendly smile and prepared for a compliment. 'I know your face. Didn't I meet you at a Whist Drive at Barker's?' One compliment I constantly receive has become rather tedious. People are always telling me what a beautiful performance I gave in *The Ladykillers*. Beautiful, certainly, but not mine. The laurels belong to that dear actress, Katie Johnson, who after a long life spent in playing supporting parts, leapt suddenly into fame. When I congratulated her she said modestly, 'Oh, my dear, it's only because I'm so old.' Films were written for her but she died before she could make them. I hope she is amused and perhaps pleased to know I'm keeping her fame alive even so vicariously. I'm afraid nowadays when receiving these undeserved congratulations, I just say, 'Yes it was a good film, wasn't it?' and leave it at that.

Of course the theatre is my first love. But when discussing it I've said many a time that my feeling for it is rather like being in love with someone whom you don't really *like*. He's exasperating but you can't give him up. My second choice, television, hasn't the same effect. I'm much more objective about it. All the same, as the day of transmission approaches, I become obsessed with one thought: *I can't act*. I forget the simplest lines, usually one in particular. I invent tunes to fit it, I create a personal Pelmanism by means of initials. I wish I could faint or even die before the performance, but up to date I've done neither. Both on television and in the theatre I'm accompanied by three phantoms: one is doing the acting for me, one keeping a desperate eye on the invisible script, and the third whispering, 'Yes I've said that. Now what?' And they are all of them *me*.

Radio always comes as a blessed respite after a long session of television. I've already spoken of its attraction. Early in my career, Martyn C Webster, one of radio's chief directors, gave me an interview. 'What sort of parts do you enjoy best?' he asked. 'Mad people,' I promptly replied. And sure enough, the first part he offered me was that of a super-eccentric actress in a play that later was made into a film called *Tread Softly*. It wasn't nearly so good as the radio version and when I saw it I was rather dismayed by my own performance.

143

I worked for Martyn in several other radio plays and always enjoyed his very special sense of humour. Looking back on my early acting days, humour at rehearsal seems to have been conspicuously absent. I'm all in favour of discipline but a little laughter does help the work along. It has a leavening effect, bringing actor and director much closer. Perhaps the actor-manager of the period gave the proceedings something of their solemnity. The present-day director is usually young and not too consciously superior, or maybe we ourselves are more relaxed.

There is much talk about the differences between acting for stage, screen, television and radio. Personally I don't believe there is a great gulf fixed between any of them. It is only a question of degrees of projection; the method is much the same. Many actors go in for protracted homework. I find too much of this embarrassing. Having put together the bones of a character, the flesh begins to grow on it during the process of rehearsing and learning the lines. You begin to *be* the person. To my way of thinking, a lot of intense homework can destroy that deep sense of *being*. But that is just my own private approach; many people will disagree.

Now that television and radio have gained a far wider scope the gulf between them and the stage has diminished so as to be almost imperceptible. There are, however, one or two important dissimilarities. The relentless television records every eyeblink. The slightest exaggeration of facial expression or gesture comes over to the viewer, any insincerity is glaringly evident, whereas the stage permits more expansion and in films, editing can perform miracles of repair. Sound radio is also a merciless recorder. A faulty inflexion, however small, is apparent, while in the theatre it is more quickly forgotten. One of the reasons why television is perhaps the most exacting of the four media is the necessity for absolute truth. Concentration, too, is essential, you can't let go for an instant. I think this challenge is one of its great attractions. I'm all for economy in acting: the minimum of facial expression and gesture. This must be my only concession to economy, for in most other matters my extravagance, is—well, extravagant.

In the theatre, directors are usually experienced; in television you are often faced with a director young and new to his job, and that makes you distrustful. But I nearly always find that even the least experienced can contribute something to your performance if only you look out for it. 'The readiness is all', or at least something to be reckoned with.

Thank Heaven I'm rarely the victim of type-casting, though I must admit that a good many sweet old ladies come my way who constantly fall a prey to murderously-inclined gentlemen. I really do prefer a part with a bite to it. Pure comedy, which nearly all actors seem to prefer, I find extremely exacting. It's so much easier to wring tears from an audience than laughter. All the same I do enjoy working with real comedians, though the presence of a live audience in the studio is terribly distracting to me. It was my good fortune to be in several sketches with Tony Hancock, that superb artist as capable of drawing tears from his viewers as any accepted tragedian. His death left a blank that nobody can fill. Frankie Howerd and Dick Emery are two other delicious comedians. I've always found that these so-called comics have a beautifully serious side to their art, and another thing about them—they are generous and responsive and never give you the feeling of inferiority. In fact this warmth and bigness of heart goes for most people of the theatre. I think there is less small-mindedness in my profession than in most others. Most of my dearest friends are actors and actresses, many of them of forty or even fifty years' standing.

To revert for a moment to one particularly dear old friend whom I first knew when I was a student in the Benson Company: Baliol Holloway. I have spoken of him earlier in these memoirs. What a fascinating book the story of his life would have made. I used to get him to tell me tales of his early years in a company run by Mrs Bandmann-Palmer, a name unknown to any but a bygone generation. Even I hadn't heard of her until Bay regaled me with anecdotes of the strange woman who paid out tiny salaries with a grudging hand, to the accompaniment of scathing criticism. Linen, in need of laundering would come under her vocal scrutiny, but what young actor on thirty shillings a week could run to a clean shirt for every performance?

For a long time Bay and Emil, his wife, were the stars of Benson's South Company. I believe their joint weekly salaries reached the height of about eight pounds. How they contrived to save anything seems miraculous, but save they did. I'm sure that those early days were among the happiest of Bay's life. Later on he achieved fame in London and New York: the success of his Iago when he co-starred with Walter Hampden, himself an Old Bensonian, seemed to leave him unmoved. When at last, old, much enfeebled and ever mourning the loss of Emil, his memory began to fail, he still retained his glorious sense of humour. Sometimes when I came to see him he would chant snatches of his favourite Gilbert and Sullivan in a voice remarkably young and vigorous. Two of his closest friends, Elizabeth Jenkins and Penelope Turing, were constantly with him during his last years, and were his great consolation. He died in April, 1967 and we all mourned him. I should like to quote a few lines from a little tribute I wrote to his memory, part of which appeared in *The Stage*:

'We were walking up the flower-bordered pathway leading to the "Actors' Church" where we gathered for Bay's Memorial Service; his relatives, his fellow-actors and actresses, and a smattering of those who knew him only as a great actor but had never seen him off the stage. It wasn't a mournful occasion. The hymns we sang were joyful songs about praising God, and songs from Gilbert and Sullivan. There was a reading from the Book of Ecclesiasticus; "Let us now praise famous men". Donald Sinden read these lines as if they had come new-born out of his own mind. Donald Wolfit spoke about the man himself. Old memories, some of them just factual; many of them brought us to laughter, some brought us close to tears.

We came out into the April day. No "Uncertain glory", but one of those mornings that used to see him striding from Marylebone to Hampstead Heath, his dog Joey at his heels. And coming down that flower-bordered path, was it merely fancy or were there three mingling in the throng, whose faces we saw only faintly in the sunshine: Bay, and Emil, and faithful Joey. I used to tell him, "You *will* meet Emil again". And now of course he knows that what I told him is true.'

It was through contributing some small bits of information for his book *Benson and the Bensonians* that I became acquainted with John Trewin, the dramatic critic. The book gives such an authentic picture of the Benson Company that he might easily have been a Bensonian himself. And as for his wife, Wendy, but for her, I doubt if these memoirs would ever have been completed. Chapter by chapter I used to send her, and almost by return received her verdict, critical in the best possible sense; always constructive and of more help than I can say.

XII

EIGHTY YEARS ON

I think it was in May, 1968 that John Gielgud rang me up to say he was considering a new play by Alan Bennett, called *Forty Years On*. It was about a boys' school and John thought I might be suited for the part of the old Nanny. I had a clear remembrance of an absurd and delicious discourse in *Beyond the Fringe* at the Fortune Theatre, perpetrated by a young man unknown to me; that was the extent of my acquaintance with Alan Bennett. I was sent the script and was enormously impressed, still more when I received the definite offer to be in it. The play was to be put on by Toby Rowland, with whom I had worked before in *So Many Children*.

Having signed the contract, Veronica and I went off on a holiday to the Lakes, with the splendid prospect of an autumn engagement. Just before that I had flown over to Frankfurt to take part in the oddest commercial television I have ever done. Until quite recently commercial television was considered rather *infra dig*. Times have changed and besides being quite a pleasant money-maker, it is fairly enjoyable, though I think the work is harder than 'straight' television. I and two other actresses were supposed to be scouring the city in search of an ideal brand of coffee. Most of our time was spent sitting perilously in a jeep which took us rocketing up and down the town. Having found our prize, we sat quaffing the desired beverage while being whirled along, often in pouring rain. On another day we dashed off to König-stein, a village among hills just outside Frankfurt. Here I experienced almost the hardest day's work of my life, standing for hours while we posed for 'stills', accompanied always by perpetual coffee-drinking. I arrived home after four days' filming, completely worn out and more than ready for our first visit to the Lakes. We used to drive about all day in the perfect country with weather to match, and come back to our delightful hotel in Bowswater, to dine sumptuously. I've rarely spent a more perfect holiday.

About this time I decided I'd had enough of my King's Road flat. I'm an inveterate mover, and what to most people is an upheaval is to me just an exciting adventure. Veronica and I found a splendid flat in Bayswater, within walking distance of the Park; a really marvellous place and suited to our demands just then. It was large, had two of everything, even bathrooms, and here we could live our own lives and yet be very happy neighbours. While I was on tour with *Forty Years On*, prior to the London opening, Veronica heroically supervised both her move and mine, and it speaks much for her sense of fitness that on my return I found, so to speak, the time and the place and the loved one all in perfect order.

By this time I had started on the rehearsals for *Forty Years On*. On a hot August afternoon we assembled for the first read-through. Except for John (and how thankful I was for him) the cast were all strangers and I was so taken up with registering their faces that most of their names escaped me. I took Paul Eddington for the author, and wondered why the fair-haired young man sitting opposite was allowed to make so many interruptions, until it dawned on me that he was in fact the author. We were all a bit nervous and uneasy. I might have wrecked any friendship with Dorothy Reynolds by remarking fervently, 'You and I are the only women in the cast so we've *got* to be friends!' She managed to survive, however, and now she and I are friends for life—at any rate, I hope for mine, for I was the eldest member of the company by a good stretch of years. But nobody seemed to hold it against me, and as I'm a confirmed giggler, perhaps that helped to bridge the gap too. Certainly the boys, twenty-two of them, ranging in age between sixteen and twenty, appeared to regard me as one of themselves, to judge by the sweetly familiar way they treated me.

Five of us, John, Dorothy, Alan, Paul and myself, rehearsed for some days before we were joined by the boys, and then the really hard work began. Boys get easily bored, especially when under discipline. It speaks wonders for Patrick Garland, our director, that he managed to keep them interested and nearly always well-behaved during those long rehearsals. Alan kept a graphic diary, extracts from which appeared in the *Sunday Times*. Much of it concerned the later rehearsals and our opening at the Palace Theatre, Manchester, a fortnight of almost incessant rain, almost continuous rehearsing and almost constant anxiety. We were in the wrong theatre for so intimate a play, the notices weren't very encouraging, neither were the audiences. No wonder we went to Brighton feeling a bit nervous. But they liked us there, and though we were still subjected to much rehearsing, we set off for the Apollo Theatre at the end of a fortnight thoroughly encouraged. The success of *Forty Years On* is too well known to need recapitulating— a tumultuous first night, glowing reviews and a triumph for everyone concerned, most of all for our author. The play, full of delicious comedy, was permeated by a strong vein of seriousness. It astonished me that so young a writer, with no experience of either of the wars, could enter so completely into the spirit of those times. He had an uncanny sense of the idiom of that generation, or rather the two generations involved. And some of the passages contain such beauty of thought that they haunt me still. So touchingly young in many ways, he could penetrate the attitude of a period which to him was only history. Perhaps the fact that he took his Oxford degree in history may have something to do with it. The play was given an award, likewise his second play, *Getting On*, named the 'The best comedy of the year'—a misnomer in my opinion, for though the play had its moments of high comedy, basically it is deeply serious.

For John, idolised as ever, *Forty Years On* was a new departure. This rather played-out, elderly headmaster of a seedy public school was miles removed from the classic roles that brought him fame. From now onwards he would belong to the public's hearts as well as their minds. And not the public merely. The boys, while according him the respect due to his position in the theatre, all adored him. His patience and friendliness was something to admire and try to emulate. They were often noisy and irrepressible and a trial to the temper of the management: but the strongest reproof I ever heard from John was a slightly weary, 'Oh, shut up, boys!' and they always did.

Perched high in the gallery of the big school hall, the boys had long intervals of doing nothing. They used to spend much of that time in scrutinising the audience, of whom they commanded a splendid view. Their comments were often passed on to us: 'Smashing-looking bird in the fifth row.' 'Ghastly couple in the Circle, chewing gum and snogging.' 'Spotted Prince Charles in the Stalls, corpsing at all the rude jokes.' Dorothy, Paul and I also had opportunities of scanning the audience while we sat, practically invisible, at the side of the stage while other scenes were going on. There were sometimes disturbing people in front. One young man used occasionally to sit in the front row, studying a copy of the play, probably on the look-out for any discrepancies in the text. Alan used charitably to keep me amused by introducing fresh and sometimes outrageous names or bits of business, while we were sitting silently by, and of course these engendered smothered laughter from me, and whispers of 'How unprofessional!' from Dorothy, whose self-control is enviable.

Among the many plays I've been in, *Forty Years On* holds a special place. I think it was the boys. Obstreperous, affectionate, exasperating and entirely lovable, they became like the children that some of us had, and that some of us would have loved to have. I still keep in touch with many of them. Several are playing in the West End. I think most of us 'grown-ups' follow their careers.

As for the five of us principals, we became the closest of friends. So often you lose sight of those colleagues you have known intimately for a long run, but the cast of *Forty Years On* has remained almost as close as when we were in daily contact. We dine together in our special Soho restaurants; I send Alan my short stories to criticise. Poor man, so occupied with his own work, he never seems too busy to send back a valuable if sometimes scathing criticism. Paul too; he and his wife and their enchanting family are very much part of my life. He is the sort of person to whom one could confide a guilty secret and be sure of a friendly response—but so far that occasion has not arisen.

All of them such dear friends; and yet we are told that new friendships are rarely made after middle-age. I take leave to contradict that saying. In the last four years I've taken lots of new friends into my life, not all from the theatre either. One whom I am proud to claim is Neville Cardus. I met him a few years ago and found him even more fascinating in life than in the autobiography which made me one of his fans. Not long ago I heard him lecture on Sir Thomas Beecham at the Purcell Room. He spoke entirely without notes and moreover without the slightest hesitation, a marvel for any speaker but miraculous in a man of over eighty.

Working in *Forty Years On* all through the summer, one of our rare hot spells, was exhausting, with one or two commercials thrown in, to say nothing of a film, *Run a Crooked Mile*, which took up only a few days but was fraught with the usual tremors about getting to the theatre on time. One of the liabilities of filming is the abnormally early rising, though as soon as you're up and dressed, you've forgotten what time it is.

I left the Apollo at the end of August. John was scheduled to leave then, and both Dorothy and I felt our time had also come. On our last night there was a wonderful party and much present-giving. We all felt regretful at leaving our happy environment, though I must say for my own part, a year's run is about my limit. We all made promises for a speedy meeting, and went home laden with gifts and memories. I managed to snaffle three weeks' holiday; not since my schooldays had I taken such a long break. I went for ten days to Ireland, where I spent the most deliciously lazy time, eating, sleeping and taking drives about the country. Then I realised one of the ambitions of my life—a visit to Rome.

I can't begin to describe the joy of that fortnight—temperatures in the eighties, the bluest skies I've ever seen, and the glories of that glorious city. I found St Peter's a little disappointing except for the *Pietà*, beautiful beyond words. I also visited one or two picture galleries and of course the Catacombs, this last an awe-inspiring if somewhat gloomy experience. I went there by coach, the driver pointing out places of interest as we drove historically spellbound along the Appian Way; then he announced in a tone approaching reverence, 'And that house belongs to Elizabeth Taylor,' and we came down to 1969 with a bump. But the highlight of my visit was the Pope. I saw him on two occasions. Once I heard him speak in at least three languages (his English being the most difficult to follow) at a public audience in St Peter's. The second was a great occasion. A new church for Ukrainian exiles had just been built a few miles out of the city, and I had the good fortune to get an invitation to a con-celebrated Mass after which the Pope was to arrive to bless some relics. We got there at about eight in the morning and had wonderful places, though no seats; we just stood, hundreds of us, in blazing sunshine while the Mass went on, the Ukrainian Priests in glowing vestments and the crowds breathlessly awaiting the arrival of His Holiness. The Mass was very long and some of it unintelligible, but wonderfully impressive.

We had Holy Communion, those of us near the front
the barriers separating us from the church. It was stran
receiving the Host according to the Eastern Rite.

Then came the great moment. Preceded by a fleet
out-riders, curiously modern on their motor-cycles an
this mediaeval splendour, the Pope swept up to
Church in his car, standing, so that we all had a cl
view of the small, delicate figure in his scarlet cloak.
discarded this, went into the church to bless the r
and then came out to give us the Apostolic Blessin
wasn't the least aware of feeling tired, standing as we
for close on four hours, until it was all over and
Papal car had faded into the distance. We were
invited to lunch with some Italian students and
glad we were of the rest.

Walking about the streets in Rome is terrifying. 7
seems more traffic than in any other city. The pedes
weave in and out, beset by cars coming from
direction and seemingly regardless of traffic signs. I
to spend most of my time waiting to cross the roa
a wonder I ever got to the other side. I tried to pi
some Italian and managed to memorize dozens of
but verbs somehow floored me so I could nev
together a grammatical sentence. I stayed in a cha
little hotel and nearly every evening ate my din
the garden. My bedroom boasted a private ba
odd contraption in which you couldn't lie full-len
had to sit up rather precariously. I also had a
balcony. It was wonderful to look out every mor
an expanse of blue sky and three tall pine trees.
flew back to England early in October, and
settle down to television and intermittent ses
story-writing. One or two stage plays were sugge
nothing really attractive. It's no use accepting
just because the part is good, if the play isn't.

In 1970, the year of Dickens's Centenary
Brahms and Ned Sherrin put on a delightful pro
in which I played Miss La Creevy. Margaret Ru

was the original choice, but illness prevented her from doing it and I was called in at very short notice. I was proud to take her place, an actress whose unique personality endeared her to everyone.

It was good to be once more with Sybil in the Dickens programme. She played his mother and as always was right on the ball, though I know she was in pain most of the time. Sybil is a species of King Charles's head with me. Whenever I suffer an interview I nearly always find myself talking about her. She is my *beau ideal*, or should I say *belle*? Some time ago she slipped on a wet pavement and fractured her elbow, but she was committed to go to a matinée of *Saint Joan* at the Mermaid Theatre, and go she did. Lately she has been making a splendid recovery from an illness that overtook her while staying in Dublin with her son Christopher. Many people of her age would have given in. Not Sybil! As soon as she was well enough to be discharged from hospital she flew back to England, and shortly afterwards was at St Paul's, Covent Garden, 'the Actor's Church', at the unveiling of a plaque in memory of Lewis. Lewis's death in May 1969 left a blank in the theatre that will never be filled. We all cherish the remembrance of his Memorial Service in the Abbey, where Sybil, a gallant figure in white, headed the procession, and her son John, and John Gielgud gave beautiful readings. I think it would have warmed Lewis's heart to see that gathering of his family and such loving friends—perhaps he was looking on, I shouldn't be surprised. I'm sure he must have been an exultant spectator on the occasion of the gala performance at the Haymarket Theatre, last October, when practically all theatrical London gathered to celebrate Sybil's ninetieth birthday. It was a most exciting and moving experience. Sybil, really glamorous in a shimmering dress, was led on to the stage and made a little speech of thanks, her voice ringing across the theatre, as young as it has ever been. Someone said, 'And all this will be happening again in another ten years!'

When I lived close to her in the King's Road we often met at the grocer's at the corner and would hold impartial discussions about Cheddar cheese and the Church, and strolling home, argue amiably over politics. I can still hear that absurdly youthful voice exclaiming, 'Don't be a fool, Nick!' and I'm transported back to the Vic and the Express Dairy. 'Age cannot wither nor custom stale' the friendship that began half a century ago.

I was asked the other day to name the people who had been the greatest influence for good in my life. Without hesitation I named Sybil and Lewis Casson, John Gielgud, Christopher Fry, two very dear Catholic priests, my sister Elaine and my niece Veronica. Each one for a different reason, but with one thing in common: their unquenchable goodness.

To return to my own story. In the summer of 1970 I was in one of Brian Rix's Sunday night television shows in the theatre. It was an alarming experience, faced with an audience and an army of cameras for a one-night stand. It was the hottest day of a long, hot summer and the play, *Lord Arthur Savile's Crime*, meant Victorian dresses of heavy silk and velvet, to say nothing of wigs and every kind of warmth-inducing prop. The play, an adaptation of a short story by Oscar Wilde, is an absurd and delicious extravaganza and I thoroughly enjoyed it, in spite of the customary nervous tension. It was great fun acting with Brian Rix and his wife Elspet, with Wallie Douglas directing in an atmosphere of unfailing good-humour. Soon after that I was in two Irish television plays for Granada, Manchester. One of these necessitated flying to Cork for a couple of days' filming. I was an eccentric old woman who has come into money. In one scene I had to attempt to cross the crowded St Patrick Street, waving my umbrella to try to stop the traffic. As I stood on the curb, up came a youth who courteously offered to see me across. He must have put me down as an eccentric indeed when I replied, 'Oh, I don't really want to cross, I'm only pretending.'

A little later that year I took part in a most enchanting television film, *Reunion*. We filmed in a village just outside Chichester. Thorley Walters and I were a mother and son who had been parted since his babyhood. Our dramatic encounter took place on the banks of a dried-up estuary, talking all the while, but never really acknowledging our relationship. Though we are aware of it, we still keep the matter unexplained. For the film we were lent a charming cottage belonging to a retired Naval Commander, where the final meeting took place: a perfect setting. While in the village our work was constantly interrupted by villagers going about their business on foot and in cars. One irate driver exclaimed, 'You may be the BBC but we live in the village and have our own work to do.' The photography of the film was exquisite. I saw it in colour and the delicate grey and blue of sky and country toned beautifully with the gentle pathos of the story. The director, Gavin Millar, was splendid to work with.

The following summer I flew over to Stockholm to do a commercial advertising an insurance company. I enjoyed this, as besides doing the thing in mime, I had the chance of seeing something of the country. We did most of the filming in the old part of the town: fascinating cobbled streets flanked by beautiful houses. Walking up and down on the cobbles was hard on the feet, and I had to do this for four days on end. Although it was mid-June, it was frightfully cold with a wind blowing, I'm convinced, straight from the North Pole. During the film I was interviewed (in English) and later on was sent the result in a Swedish newspaper. I was unable to translate more than about three words, so for all I know, the finished product may not have been complimentary. Certainly the accompanying photograph was not.

Earlier in these memoirs I spoke of my father's chaplaincy in Gothenburg. As it wasn't far from Stockholm I went over for the week-end after my work was finished, hoping I might find the English Church still in existence. Miraculously it was: just as it had been in my father's day. I made the acquaintance of the English Chaplain who took me over the Church and showed me a panel bearing the names of former clergy, including 'Mr Nicholson'. It was a beautiful and moving experience to find myself in the very place where my parents had spent so many years, long before I was born.

And then I came home to more work, new friendships and a golden autumn. I think I've already said I'm a compulsive mover. By this time the Bayswater flat had begun to lose its allure both for Veronica and myself. Though very spacious and comfortable it was terribly dark, even in summer electric light was nearly always necessary; and I had a yearning to be in Chelsea again. A stroke of good fortune, amounting to a miracle, led me to my new home, just off Sloane Square, where the Royal Court Theatre is my 'local'. To be in a play there would be the height of luxury. I feel that this flat will really be my last, until I'm called to a more permanent Home.

Not long after I'd settled down in Chelsea, Christmas came round again; the most blessed season of the year except Easter, the Church's highest festival. It's the fashion to say, 'Oh, Christmas, I'm tired out before it starts.' Of course you're tired, but how worthwhile it is! You think you've completed your annual list only to find you're rushing round at the eleventh hour, scooping up gifts you've forgotten to buy, collecting the turkey, laying in an extra stock of cards, and staggering home under a load of holly, fingers lacerated but temper unimpaired. What does it all amount to, asks the cynic. It amounts to 'Come all ye faithful'. Midnight Mass has kept you up into the small hours. You spend a leisurely Christmas morning and then it's time to think about the dinner.

I love Christmas. Every year it comes as an awakening, like the coming of Spring. My mind leaps back to

Svea Lodge; to Church in the morning and Mrs Muggins at night. Veronica and I decorate our pint-size Christmas tree, exchange our presents, and then prepare for the evening when a few cherished friends come to dinner. Only Antonia, Veronica and myself are left out of our large family. Even if we look back wistfully over the years, Christmas still holds its promise and it never fails.

There are statistics estimating how many hours of our lives are spent in sleeping. I am not acquainted with the figures, but I have been wondering about the percentage of hours we spend in wasting time. I have an uneasy feeling that mine is distressingly high. I cast my mind back over the years and feel abashed. After my first visit to Rome I determined to study Italian. I took down the address of an Italian teacher. For three years she has been awaiting me. How often I've planned an afternoon at the National Gallery, the Victoria and Albert Museum, Ham House. Just as often I've put my feet up and done *The Times* Crossword instead. All these omissions have been simply personal losses; but I am guilty of something more serious: neglecting to call on sick or lonely people. I'll go tomorrow, I tell myself, and awake, sometimes literally, to the fact that tomorrow has extended itself to tomorrow week. How much time have I left to make up those wasted hours? Perhaps some of my years in Purgatory will be devoted to broadening my mind and loving my neighbour.

Quite lately I paid another visit to Rome in circumstances very different from those in 1969. I flew over for forty-eight hours, to make a test for an Italian film in which I was to be the only English woman—a distinguished and rich old lady who spent a few weeks in Rome every year, in order to indulge her passion for the essentially Italian card-game—Scopoke. Rome was beautiful in its early Spring dress, with peach blossom and mimosa already glowing in the streets. I enjoyed my brief stay, although it meant two days' hard work, being fitted for temporary costumes and then making the rather nerve-shaking test. Alas, the result wasn't in my favour. The verdict was, 'Too gentle for the part of the irascible old dame.' Gentle! But I'm not. Appearances have always been against me. To misquote *Hamlet*. 'God has given me one face but how I wish he'd made me another!' Discussing my failure with a candid friend, he remarked, 'They should have got on to me. I could have told them you're a monster.' Perhaps I'm something between the two. It's very true that in my youth I was inclined to be hard, resentful, intolerant and supremely selfish. Now that I'm old I like to think that time has softened the sharp edges, or is it that life is so much easier that I can afford a little more charity? Youth *is* a sad time, in spite of all its attendant joys. It is a constant battle and so often a losing one. And now 'The strife is o'er, the battle done.' That is an old Easter message. In our mortal life maybe the battle is never really done, but there is often a long truce.

Not long ago I was being interviewed in BBC 'Woman's Hour', and one of the questions put to me was, 'What time of your life would you consider the happiest?' I'd no hesitation in replying, 'Now.' My questioner was surprised. I think most people like to look back on some halcyon period of their youth and possibly over-glamourise it. Of course I've had halcyon days, lots of them, but I find a certain satisfaction and peace in what are known as one's declining years. I can take more interest in the lives of others than I ever could when life was a pulsating drama with myself as chief performer. Happiness can be so ephemeral, personal happiness, I mean. I used, in moments of ecstasy, to think, 'Don't let this go on in case it stops.' There seems no sense in that, but I think it was because I was always afraid of losing the exquisite moment. Even the prospect of Life Everlasting I apprehend with something of that same foreboding. Eternity! Of course we can't compre- hend it, but my limited intelligence somehow finds it frightening. 'For ever and ever' without even 'Amen' to finish it off. I think I'd like to be a sort of Sleeping Beauty in reverse: experience perfect happiness for a hundred years and then go to sleep for ever and ever. Someone said to me only a day or two ago, 'I believe in a hereafter but I'd rather not.' And he quoted Addison's line: 'Eternity! That pleasing, dreadful thought.' It comes near to expressing my own.

As I've said before, young people have a tremendous charm for me. Their problems, so like my own in the past, seem to bring my youth closer and make me forget my age—something that doesn't worry me except for the regret that there must be so little time left. Now that we are growing so familiar with Space, should Time seem so important? Recently the whole world was Moon-struck. Strikes, work-to-rule, even our own domestic problems faded into insignificance beside the stupendous achievement of the astronauts. The Moon, once faraway and romantic, lost its mystery and became so accessible that it seemed in the not too distant future we shall be saying, 'This week Theatre Royal, Brighton, next week, The Moon.'

I'm afraid I'm a reactionary. These men in their space-suits, taking their perilous walks among the rocks and craters, seem to me to be intruding on the privacy of that legendary and solitary inhabitant, The Man in the Moon. Is it possible he's rather peevish at having his privacy disturbed? Perhaps he has a notice on his front door: 'No Callers.'

To come down to Earth again, for my own part, the past few years have been very rewarding with plenty of work and only brief holidays. So, as I write these last lines, overlooking a vast expanse of London, with a glimpse of the Victoria Tower and Westminster Cathedral on one side, and on the other the friendly winking of the Post Office Tower, I've travelled as far as the present moment. I suppose I've achieved some measure of success, though I've been an unconscionably long time about it and I can't say that the travel has always been hopeful. But now I believe I've swept up most of the crumbs from my Chameleon's Dish and my turbulent mind is more or less at rest. All the same, it's a little disturbing to feel about twenty-three when your contemporaries have settled down to the dignity and poise consonant with old age. I still wait for the telephone to ring. I still don't know what I'll be doing or where I'll be in the next few months.

On looking back I like to think that this story of my varied life in the theatre may encourage any young people who are finding their early years difficult, though in these days there are many more opportunities of earning a living than when I started.

And now, having arrived, so to speak, I haven't much more to say. On reviewing this story it seems to take on the semblance of those temperature charts of ups and downs. In and out of love, in and out of work; so erratic a chart would cause alarm to any hospital nurse. But through it all one love has remained constant: my love of life.

Today the chart shows a pretty even temperature—ninety-eight, point four, let us say. Just as well, I suppose. But sometimes I picture it taking a sudden surge upwards again, on that problematic anniversary when I may receive the Queen's telegram: not that I covet the grandeur of that. It's just that I'd simply love to live to be a hundred.

Spring, 1973.

Index

167

169